Biblical Interpretation in the Early Church

Sources of Early Christian Thought

A series of new English translations of patristic
texts essential to an understanding of Christian
theology
WILLIAM G. RUSCH, EDITOR

The Christological Controversy
Richard A. Norris, Jr., translator/editor

The Trinitarian Controversy
William G. Rusch, translator/editor

Theological Anthropology
J. Patout Burns, S.J., translator/editor

The Early Church and the State
Agnes Cunningham, SSCM, translator/editor

Biblical Interpretation in the Early Church

Translated and Edited by
KARLFRIED FROEHLICH

FORTRESS PRESS
PHILADELPHIA

———————

Library of Congress Cataloging in Publication Data

Main entry under title:

Biblical interpretation in the Early Church.

(Sources of early Christian thought)
Translated from the Greek, Hebrew, Latin, and Syriac.
Bibliography: p.
1. Bible—Criticism, interpretation, etc.—History—
Early church ca. 30–600. 2. Bible—Criticism, interpretation, etc.—History—Early church, ca. 30–600—
Sources. I. Froehlich, Karlfried. II. Series.
BS500.B55 1985   220.6'09'015   84-47922
ISBN 0-8006-1414-3

———————

K961E84   Printed in the United States of America   1–1414

Contents

Series Foreword

Christianity has always been attentive to historical fact. Its motivation and focus have been, and continue to be, the span of life of one historical individual, Jesus of Nazareth, seen to be a unique historical act of God's self-communication. The New Testament declares that this Jesus placed himself within the context of the history of the people of Israel and perceived himself as the culmination of the revelation of the God of Israel, ushering into history a new chapter. The first followers of this Jesus and their succeeding generations saw themselves as part of this new history. Far more than a collection of teachings or a timeless philosophy, Christianity has been a movement in, and of, history, acknowledging its historical condition and not attempting to escape it.

Responsible scholarship now recognizes that Christianity has always been a more complex phenomenon than some have realized, with a variety of worship services, theological languages, and structures of organization. Christianity assumed its variegated forms on the anvil of history. There is a real sense in which history is one of the shapers of Christianity. The view that development has occurred within Christianity during its history has virtually universal acceptance. But not all historical events had an equal influence on the development of Christianity. The historical experience of the first several centuries of Christianity shaped subsequent Christianity in an extremely crucial manner. It was in this initial phase that the critical features of the Christian faith were set: a vocabulary was created, options of belief and practice were accepted or rejected. Christianity's understanding of its God and of the person of Christ, its worship life, its communal structure, its understanding of the human condition, all were largely resolved in this early period known as the time of the church fathers or the patristic church (A.D. 100–700). Because this is the case, both those individuals who bring a faith commitment to Christianity and those interested in it as a major religious and historical phenomenon must have a special regard for what happened to the Christian faith in these pivotal centuries.

The purpose of this series is to allow an English-reading public to gain firsthand insights into these significant times for Christianity by making available in a modern, readable English the fundamental sources which chronicle how Christianity and its theology attained their normative character. Whenever possible, entire patristic writings or sections are presented. The varying points of view within the early church are given their opportunity to be heard. An introduction by the translator and editor of each volume describes the context of the documents for the reader.

Hopefully these several volumes will enable their readers to gain not only a better understanding of the early church but also an appreciation of how Christianity of the twentieth century still reflects the events, thoughts, and social conditions of this earlier history.

It has been pointed out repeatedly that the problem of doctrinal development within the church is basic to ecumenical discussion today. If this view is accepted, along with its corollary that historical study is needed, then an indispensable element of true ecumenical responsibility has to be a more extensive knowledge of patristic literature and thought. It is with that urgent concern, as well as a regard for a knowledge of the history of Christianity, that Sources of Early Christian Thought is published.

WILLIAM G. RUSCH

I.

Introduction

Patristic hermeneutics (from the Greek *hermēneuein,* to explain, interpret) concerns itself with the developing principles and rules for a proper understanding of the Bible in the early Christian church. The *principles* reflect the theological framework in which the biblical writings were interpreted by different groups and individuals at various times; they always included the basic conviction that God's revelation in Jesus Christ was central to God's plan of salvation (*oikonomia*), but they left room for different readings of major themes such as Israel and the church, eschatology, ethics, even Christology, anthropology, and soteriology. The *rules* reflect the methodology by which the language of biblical revelation was scrutinized so that it would yield insight into God's *oikonomia* and its ramifications for the life of the community; they were often taken over from the literary culture of the surrounding world but were then developed into new, creative paradigms of literary analysis. Rules and principles are intimately related. Thus, while the selections in this volume illustrate primarily the development of the rules, they shed much light on the principles also. They show, on the one hand, how biblical language determined theology and, on the other, how theological presuppositions shaped the reading of the Bible. It was in the hermeneutical circle of biblical text, tradition, and interpretation that Christian theology as a whole took shape.

JEWISH BACKGROUND

The Jewish Canon

From the start, Christians shared the Holy Scriptures of the Jews. As it had been for Jesus, Scripture for them was first and

1

foremost the collection of authoritative Jewish writings which had its center in the law (*torâ*) and the prophets (*nĕbî'îm*) while a number of "writings" (*kĕtubîm*) or hagiographa, especially the psalter, enjoyed authority but had varying degrees of use and acceptance among different Jewish groups. At the beginning of the Christian era there was no closed and fully defined Jewish canon as yet, although the core had been established for a long time. The delimitation of the canon was probably connected with the events of the Jewish revolt against Rome in A.D. 66/73 and the subsequent loss of the center of Jewish life in Jerusalem. We know of meetings of rabbis in Jabne (Jamnia) on the Palestinian coast at the end of the first century where the authority of certain books was a topic of discussion; around A.D. 95/100 the Jewish historian Josephus made reference to the final canon in twenty-four parts (thirty-nine books) including *torâ*, prophets, and thirteen "writings." The dominant viewpoint in the rabbinical decision was that of the Pharisaic group which subsequently became the rallying point for Jewish identity in the time of dispersion and persecution.

The Pharisaic reduction of normative books ended a very different trend in the preceding three centuries. During the troubled times under the Seleucid ruler Antiochus IV Epiphanes (176–164 B.C.) the prophetic literature found increased attention in Jewish circles that understood their time as the end time and their communities as the remnant of the true Israel. From the Maccabean period on, new apocalyptic writings appeared in ever-growing numbers and were eagerly seized by the common people as well as groups like the Essenes with their sectarian communities in Palestine and elsewhere. At the time of Jesus, therefore, the later Pharisaic canon was by no means standard. If one considers that for the Sadducees scriptural authority rested in the five books of Moses only, while the canon of the Qumran sect or the Septuagint (the Greek Bible) included additional books often apocalyptic in nature, the Pharisaic canon appears as a compromise endorsing as normative neither a minimum nor a maximum of the available literature in use among Jews. It does reveal a bias against the newer apocalyptic and pseudepigraphic literature and its use in sectarian circles, perhaps including the Christians.

Jewish Hermeneutics

While the final delimitation of an authoritative canon was a fairly late development, biblical interpretation in Judaism had a long and varied history. Jewish hermeneutics, like all hermeneutics of sacred books, was determined by the theological framework and the goals of the actual community in which these Scriptures played a normative role. Viewed from this angle, three Jewish groups are important for a consideration of the early Christian development: the rabbis, the Qumran sect, and the various strands of Diaspora Judaism.

The Rabbis

Rabbinic hermeneutics, the dominant hermeneutics in later Judaism, had the purpose of making Scripture available as the record of God's revealed will for the guidance of Jewish life. It drew on the rich oral tradition of the earlier interpreters of the Law, that is, the scribes of the generations after Ezra and the teachers of the period after the Maccabean revolt (*tannā'îm*), a tradition which eventually issued in the great written collections of Mishnah, Gemara, and Talmud in Christian times. At first the tradition of oral law had developed parallel to the transmission of *torâ*, but when its authority met with doubt, for example, among the Sadducees, the essential unity of *torâ* and tradition, written and oral law, had to be demonstrated. Rabbinical exegetes claimed that both went back to God's revelation to Moses on Mount Sinai. But the mere claim was not enough; its validity had to be proved from the biblical texts themselves. Thus, methods of coordinating text, tradition, and contemporary application developed which, while they seem strange to modern eyes, took the challenge seriously.

This principle of necessary coordination formed the context for the emergence of several sets of rabbinical rules (*middôt*) for biblical interpretation. Their exact history is hard to trace because even the Mishnah in its earliest written form is of a relatively late date, and authentic recollection is hard to distinguish from legendary adaptation. The rabbinic commentary (*midrăs*) on the biblical Book of Numbers, known as Sifra and dating back to the second century C.E., starts out with a tradition (*bāraytā'*) attributing a set of thirteen *middôt* to Rabbi Ishmael (see chapter II). Whether the tradition can be traced to the historical Ishmael who lived in the early second century or represents a composite list of early rules is a matter of debate. It is clear, however, that these rules assumed considerable importance. Some later authorities regarded them as part of the oral *torâ* given to Moses on Mount Sinai; to this day, the thirteen *middôt* are recited in the daily Morning Prayer. Their purpose is quite clear. They are meant to facilitate the solution of legal questions and problems of daily living. In order to do this, they offer a method of logical deduction from the biblical text that pays attention to certain structural elements and rhetorical devices. The method works by word association as the examples make clear; one passage recalls another because of a particular word or phrase, and the combination yields the proof for a specific traditional solution to a legal problem. In contrast to Rabbi Aqiba who assumed a mysterious revelation behind every detail of the sacred text, Rabbi Ishmael formulated the principle: "The *torâ* speaks in the language of men." His rules indeed display a sober sense of rational textual analysis.

A briefer and probably older set of seven *middôt* was attributed to the famous Rabbi Hillel, an older contemporary of Jesus (ca. 20 B.C. to A.D. 15). Legend claims that Hillel rose to fame when he solved the question whether the Passover may be sacrificed on a Sabbath by appealing to several of these rules before members of the Sanhedrin. Our text from Sifra alludes to the episode. D. Daube has convincingly argued that all these rules reflect the logic and methods of Hellenistic grammar and forensic rhetoric. Legal teaching (*halākâ*, from the Hebrew *hlk*, to walk) was not, however, the only meaning derived from the holy texts. A later expansion of Rabbi Ishmael's rules into thirty-two *middôt* under the name of Rabbi Eliezer ben Josē shows that the texts were also searched for more general edifying applications (*haggādâ*). Here, the inclusion of such techniques as paronomasia, gematria (i.e., the computation of the numerical value of letters), and *nōtrikon* (the breaking up of one word into two or more) indicates the underlying conviction that deeper mysteries are hidden in the very words of Scripture. On this basis, there certainly is a case for rabbinical allegorism.

The Qumran Community

The second form of Jewish interpretive theory is known to us through the Dead Sea Scrolls, the library of the Essene community of Qumran which flourished in the post-Maccabean period and perished at the time of the Roman wars. The Qumran group was characterized by a strong consciousness of end time. Rejecting the Temple cult of Jerusalem and its priestly guardians, it understood itself as the remnant of Israel waiting for the final revelation of God in the age to come. For these people, biblical interpretation had the purpose of reading the signs of the time and providing guidance for living in it. Its most characteristic feature was *pešer* exegesis (from the Aramaic *pšr*, to interpret), a form of commentary which applied biblical texts, especially from prophetic books, to the immediate situation of the sect and its struggles. The authoritative key to the mystery (*rāz*) hidden in the text was in the hands of their leader, the "Teacher of Righteousness," whom they regarded, like Moses and Ezra, as one of the inspired mediators of God's revelation. Thus, while the application of *torâ* was still the goal of the hermeneutical endeavor, it was the *torâ* of the end time which the group was seeking. With this eschatological preoccupation the center of Scripture was moving away from the *torâ* to the prophets and to the revelational authority of the Teacher of Righteousness.

Diaspora Judaism

A third form of Jewish hermeneutics was prominent among Jews of the Diaspora, especially the active Jewish community in Alexandrian Egypt. It is exemplified by the prolific exegetical work of Philo (ca. 20 B.C. to A.D. 50), an older contemporary of Jesus like Hillel, whose writings survived due, in large measure, to later Christian sympathies. In the cultured atmosphere of the

Hellenistic capital with its schools and their interest in ancient texts, Jews were able not only to live by their traditional norms but to make the Law attractive to the Greek religious mind. It was in Egypt that bold apologists for the Jewish cause claimed nothing less than the dependence of the Greek sages on the older wisdom of Moses and the prophets.

The Jewish canon of Alexandria was the Septuagint, which in its core of *torâ*, prophets, and psalms coincided with the later Pharisaic canon but included among the hagiographa books such as Judith, Tobit, 1 and 2 Esdras, and Ecclesiasticus. Protestants today regard these books as "Apocrypha," while Roman Catholics retain them as deuterocanonical because the canon of the Latin Vulgate was following the Septuagint. Among the defenders of this Greek translation, the rabbinical understanding of the written and oral law as revelation given to Moses on Mount Sinai was defined more precisely by a Hellenistic concept of inspiration which assumed direct divine influence upon the writing of the sacred texts ranging from a writer's ecstasy to verbal dictation (cf. Philo, *On the Special Laws* I.65; IV.49). From such inspiration Hellenistic scholarship derived the notion of a deeper truth, an intended spiritual sense (*hyponoia*) of the human words that the interpreter has to uncover by means of "allegory," allowing the text to say something else from what the words seem to suggest. Thus, the texts of the ancient poets such as Homer and Hesiod, who were regarded as God-inspired, were scrutinized for the deeper cosmological or ethical truth contained in them under the veil of the mythical narrative. In fact, the claim of divine inspiration gave these venerable texts an oracular quality which allowed their retention as normative for the present generation and stimulated much creative imagination not only in the production of new, deliberately allegorical poetry but also in the interpretation of old texts.

In this climate Jewish apologetics promoted the legend that the Greek translation of their ancient holy books was the work of seventy or seventy-two inspired elders endorsed by the Alexandrian Jewish community in the third century B.C. (*Letter of Aristeas*, ca. 130 B.C.). Philo quoted an even more dramatic version: Though working in total isolation, each one in his cell, the elders emerged with the same choice of words and phrases "as if a teacher was dictating to each of them invisibly" (*Life of Moses* II.37). For centuries the authority of the inspired Septuagint outweighed the authority of the Hebrew text among Jews of the Diaspora and Christians who told the miraculous story of its origin in ever more colorful detail. Even Augustine of Hippo at first resisted Jerome's effort to translate the Latin Bible from the "Hebrew truth," being convinced that the Septuagint's divine origin made it superior and more suitable for Christian use than the Hebrew Bible (*Epistle* 28.2; 71.4; *On Christian Doctrine* II.xv.22; *City of God* XVIII.43).

Philo was familiar with halakic and haggadic traditions deriving from the scribes and the rabbis and was far from wanting to discourage literal adherence to the Torah (*On the Migration of Abraham* 89–94). But in the tradition of Alexandrian Jewish apologetics he also found the philosophical truths of Stoic ethics and Platonic cosmology behind the "impossibilities," "impieties," and "absurdities" of the biblical stories. By carefully searching the inspired text for clues such as contradictions, peculiar expressions, etymologies, mysterious numbers, and so forth, the exegete could unravel the real teaching God intended to convey, a teaching that Philo thought coincided with the best of the philosophical tradition of his time. In his multipartite commentary on Genesis and Exodus texts, Philo unfolded a wealth of critical insight and imaginative allegorization. For him, the two creation accounts in Genesis 1 and 2 spoke of two different human natures, the heavenly (Gen. 1:27) and the material (Gen. 2:7). God planting a garden in Eden meant his implanting terrestrial virtue in the human race. The river going out from Eden denoted goodness, its four heads the cardinal virtues: Pison stands for prudence, Gihon for courage, Tigris for temperance, Euphrates for justice. What the story of Abraham and Sarah explained was the relation of mind and virtue. Like his Jewish and Greek predecessors, Philo used a Platonic anthropological dichotomy as the model for his hermeneutical principle: the literal meaning of the sacred text is its body, the deeper spiritual and philosophical understanding is its soul.

CHRISTIAN BEGINNINGS

Jesus

The earliest Christian sources reflect the use of all three types of Jewish hermeneutics. According to the evangelists, the words of Jesus himself contain evidence that he used rabbinical rules like those of Hillel and Ishmael (e.g., Matt. 6:26; Mark 2:25–28; John 7:23; 10:34–36). The evangelists also portray his scriptural interpretation as closely resembling the authoritative eschatological *pešer* of the Qumran community; this is evident in the antitheses of the Sermon on the Mount ("You have heard that it was said . . . but I say unto you"), but also in the summary of his first sermon at Nazareth: "Today this Scripture has been fulfilled in your hearing" (Luke 4:21). Moreover, there are traces of deliberate allegory in his parables even though these may have been enhanced by the evangelists and may have followed Jewish precedent (e.g., Matt. 13:3–9; 13:18–23; Mark 4:3–20; Matt. 13: 24–30; 13:37–43; cf. Judg. 9:7–15).

Paul

"Allegory"

In his famous exegesis of the story of Abraham, Sarah, and Hagar (Genesis 16 and 21), Paul uses the participle *"allēgoroumena"* (Gal. 4:24; from the Greek *allēgorein,* to speak allegorically), showing his indebtedness to the terminology of Hellenistic rhetoric at this point. It seems that his use of the term and the method (cf. 1 Cor. 9:9–10) encouraged later allegorizers, especially after other writings such as the *Epistle to the Hebrews* or the *Epistle of Barnabas* promoted a more systematic polemical allegorization of the Law. Paul's scriptural interpretation reveals also familiarity with the rabbinical *middôt* (e.g., *qal wāḥōmer*: Rom. 5:15–21; 2 Cor. 3:7–18; *gĕzērâ šāwâ*: Rom. 4:1–12; *kelāl ûpĕrāt*: Rom. 13:8–10; cf. Longenecker, pp. 117–18) and with the logic of *pešer* exegesis. This last point is of particular importance.

The Hermeneutical Center

Paul, of course, did not share the hermeneutical principles of the Qumran sect but, as so many Jews of his time, he shared the conviction of living in the time of God's final revelation. This revelation had come to him personally as a new understanding of the role of Jesus and of his own mission in God's plan for the end time (Gal. 1:12–16). For him, as for the members of the Qumran sect, the hermeneutical center of Scripture was moving from the *torâ* to the prophetic message. The fulfillment of messianic prophecy in the coming, death, and resurrection of Jesus made the Jewish Scriptures the book of the Christians, the essential key to their understanding of the events which had taken place among the disciples of the first generation (1 Cor. 15:3–4). A new reading of God's history with his people was emerging which contrasted with the old reading like Spirit and Letter, even life and death (2 Cor. 3:6ff.).

Typology

The hermeneutical principle for Paul had changed, and with it the rules were changing also. In several places he tells his readers that what was written was written "for our sakes" (1 Cor. 9:9; 10:11; Rom. 4:24; 15:4). At first glance, these applications may simply reflect procedures of the haggadic Midrash. In 1 Cor. 10:1–11 Paul draws on midrashic traditions connected with Exod. 17:5–6; Num. 21:16–17; Deut. 32:1–7. But his new hermeneutical principle gives the interpretation a new framework comparable to that of the Qumran *pešer*. In this context Paul used the language of "type" (*typos:* 1 Cor. 10:6; Rom. 5:14; *typikōs*: 1 Cor. 10:11) which had served to denote a pattern or example elsewhere. Recognizing such "types" in Jewish Scriptures was part of the spiritual insight Christians received with their baptismal instruction for Paul: they were able to recognize the "spiritual" rock from which saving water flows and to identify the "spiritual" food and drink in the wilderness with Christian realities. Thus Paul's allegorization, like that of other early Christian writers, took the form of an eschatological typology; the events of Jewish history were read as prefiguring the events of the end time which had begun in the revelation of Jesus Christ. Later New Testament authors completed this logic. Christian baptism in 1 Peter 3:21 is treated as the "antitype" of Noah's rescue from the flood while Heb. 9:23–24 tied the same language to a Hellenistic-Platonic hermeneutics of copy and original, shadow and reality, even though its biblical basis is acknowledged (cf. Heb. 8:5 and Exod. 25:9, 40). The mixed language of allegorical typology which reads God's plan of salvation from the accounts of Israel's history, and of typological allegory which locates this salvation in the realm of truth beyond history became characteristic of Christian exegesis in the second century.

Paul's mission to the Gentiles prepared the way for this development. For hermeneutics as for other areas of inquiry, this mission was a decisive step. Emerging as a community independent of Judaism, Christians of many backgrounds now started to appropriate the Jewish Scriptures as their own, being taught to read them as a hidden witness to God's new covenant with humankind in the Lord Jesus Christ, the eternal Word of God. At the same time, the witness to the Word's appearance in history (cf. John 1:14) was taking shape in a new body of writings connected with the eyewitness generation of the apostles. To a faith centered in the person of the Logos-Savior, the prophetic witness of the old Scriptures and the apostolic witness of the new writings belonged together.

THE SECOND CENTURY
The Gnostic Challenge
Marcion

During the early decades of the second century the interpretation of the Jewish Scriptures remained the central hermeneutical task. This holds true even in the case of Marcion, whose polemically reduced Christian canon was probably the signal leading to the formation of an authoritative collection of apostolic writings among other Christians of the second century. Marcion, a reform-minded, conservative layman from Pontus who worked in the Roman congregation but later left it to start a rapidly expanding counterchurch (A.D.144), came to the conclusion that he had to reject the Jewish Scriptures as the work of a wrathful, vicious, evil God who was opposed to the God of love proclaimed by Jesus and revealed to Paul. Suspicious of the harmonizing tendency of allegory and its typological application, he declared that only "the Apostle," a polemically arranged corpus of ten Pauline Epistles, and "the Gospel," which meant the Gospel of Luke purged of Jewish contamination, were acceptable for Christian use.

Marcion and his hermeneutical principles were condemned, and the Jewish Scriptures in their Christian understanding were retained as the inspired prophetic witness to the truth of the Christian faith. They had proved to be a most effective apologetic and missionary tool. At the end of the controversy stood a normative Christian canon in two parts. But the decision against Marcion also had a disturbing consequence. By making the Jewish Scriptures resolutely a Christian book: the "Old Testament," which had only one legitimate continuation: the "New Testament," the emerging Christian movement defined itself once more in sharpest antithesis to the Jewish community. In fact, the tighter the grip of Christians on the Jewish Scriptures, the deeper the estrangement from the community of living Jews. For the patristic tradition after the triumph of Christianity, the Jews became the "people of witness" for God's wrath on unbelievers.

Valentinian Exegesis

The appropriation of the Jewish Scriptures in a Christian framework was also a main interest of Christian Gnostics to whom Christian exegesis in general owes a considerable debt. Of course, not all Gnostics were alike. One group, the Valentinians, seems to have been the first to produce commentaries on early Christian writings, especially the Gospel of John and the Pauline corpus; Origen's Commentary on the Fourth Gospel refutes the Gnostic Heracleon point by point. E. Pagels has suggested that the purpose of Valentinian exegesis was the coordination of Gnostic cosmology and soteriology with a hermeneutical grid extracted mainly from Paul's epistles. Valentinian public teaching was not meant for fleshly, "hylic" people who are lost or for "pneumatics" who grasp the spiritual fullness (*plērōma*), but for a middle group, the "psychics," who might still be saved being led from a simple literal exposition of the holy texts to the more esoteric instruction on ethical and spiritual truth.

Ptolemy's Letter to Flora

The *Letter of Ptolemy to Flora* (see chapter III) which has been preserved for us by being incorporated into an antiheretical treatise of the church father Epiphanius (*Panarion*, i.e., *Medicine Chest*, 33.iii–vii) comes from the Valentinian school. It exemplifies a sophisticated Gnostic appropriation of the Old Testament by a community which had every intention of being Christian. Ptolemy continued Valentinus's work in Rome; if he can be identified with the martyr Ptolemy of Justin's *Apology* II.2, Flora may have been the wife of his denouncer. The letter's teaching concerning the Law is meant to precede the initiation into the higher mysteries of the First Principle and its emanations (vii.8–9). It amounts to a rational critique which eliminates large sections of the Torah from Christian consideration and encourages the allegorical interpretation of others, taking its clue from the words of Jesus. Two secondary levels, the accommodations of Moses and the additions of the Elders (*deuterōsis*; cf. *Apostolic Constitutions*, I.6.3; II.5.6), must be distinguished from the Law of God which, according to Jesus' words, falls into three parts itself: One part the Savior fulfilled, one part he abrogated, and one part he left to symbolical interpretation (vi.1–4). The polemical front against mainline Christians as well as Marcionites is evident when the author attributes the Law of God neither to the highest God nor to the devil but to an intermediate power, the Demiurge, who is portrayed as a God of justice (iii.2–3; vii.3f.). Thus the Old Testament is retained but is assigned an inferior place to the higher revelation within a framework that derives its norms from the "words of the Savior" but follows the principles of a Gnostic view of reality.

The Answer: Authoritative Exegesis

Valentinianism was one of the major heresies attacked by Irenaeus of Lyon in the five books of his anti-Gnostic treatise, commonly known under the title *Against Heresies* (ca. 180). Irenaeus's polemic, like that of the apologists before him, centered on one point: Two testaments do not reveal two gods; rather, the one God who is the creator of All revealed himself in the successive history of both testaments as part of his overall plan of salvation for humankind. The coming of Christ, the Son and Logos of God, in the fullness of time removed the veil from that which could hardly be recognized as prediction and prefiguration before.

Justin Martyr and the Apologists

In his treatise, *Dialogue with Trypho the Jew* (ca. 160), Justin Martyr had made this point primarily against Jewish critics. His apologetic method was based on proof from prophecy. Drawing on real or supposed messianic prophecies from the Jewish tradition, he argued that Jesus clearly was the expected Messiah who fulfilled all the predictions of the Jewish Scriptures literally or typically. Justin's writings are a mine of information on standard Christian typology of the second century. Building upon the gospel tradition and other early Christian literature, he found all the major features of his christological creed predicted or prefigured in the details of the Old Testament text: Christ's virgin birth; his healing ministry, suffering, death, and resurrection; Christian baptism; the church. Types of the cross were of particular interest: Justin found them not only in the figure of Moses praying in the battle against Amalek (Exod. 17:10–11) or in the horns of the wild ox (Deut. 33:17) but in every stick, wood, tree mentioned in the Bible (*Dialogue* 86; 90–91). The immense range of such types is also illustrated by other contemporary writings such as the *Epistle of Barnabas* (ca. 135) or Melito of Sardis's *Paschal Homily* (later second century) which exploited the analogies of the exodus story with Christ's death and resurrection.

Irenaeus's Hermeneutical Principles

Irenaeus clearly joins this standard argumentation in our selection from *Against Heresies* IV.26 (see chapter IV). The Old Testament texts themselves speak of hidden truth that must be unlocked. Jews are reading them but do not have the explanation. Christians possess the key in the coming of Christ which unlocks all the mysteries of God's *oikonomia* from beginning to end. The early Christian sense of the apocalyptic situation widens here into the vision of a universal biblical history: Christ came "in the last times," but he came for the sake of all generations. Biblical typology points not only to his first advent but to the time of the church and to his second advent as well (IV.22; IV.33.1). The same argument refutes the Gnostics. If the Jews have no key, the Gnostics fabricate their own. Irenaeus first criticizes their hermeneutical principle: they cut up the beautiful mosaic of God's revealed economy and reassemble the pieces into their own myths (I.8.1; I.9.4). Their hermeneutical rules are no better: Gnostics see deep problems where there are none, explaining the clear and obvious by the dark and obscure (II.10). Scriptures need a Christian key, but this key must be handled by reliable interpreters. Neither the rabbis nor the Gnostic teachers fill this role. Irenaeus finds the proper authority in the presbyters who have their office through succession in an unbroken line of episcopal ordination from the apostles and their disciples, and whose life and doctrine exhibit the "charism of truth" (IV.26.2; I.10.1–2). Sound scriptural interpretation is the function of a church which must have not only tradition but the right tradition. Only such interpretation can be called true gnosis (IV.33.8).

Tertullian

R. M. Grant has called Irenaeus the "father of authoritative exegesis." Irenaeus, however, was not alone in calling for a hermeneutics of authority. The issue was posed even more sharply in Tertullian's treatise, *The Prescription* (i.e., *the demurral*) *of Heretics* (ca. 200). According to Tertullian, arguing with Gnostics about scriptural interpretation is useless. Even an agreed canon and common exegetical methods do not guarantee unambiguous results for there is always room for heretical intentions to dictate the agenda. Thus, the true battlefield is not interpretation but the very right to use Scriptures at all. Apostolic Scriptures belong to the apostolic church. The Gnostics with their claim to secret traditions have no right to use them, for only the public succession of teaching in the apostolically founded churches can be the measure of apostolicity and therefore of correct interpretation. "Correct" for Tertullian meant congruent with the Rule of Faith, the church's simple creed. Indeed, more is not necessary. "To know nothing against the Rule of Faith means to have all science" (*Prescription* 14). We meet here a profound suspicion toward a professional exegesis which made the unending search for truth a methodological principle. The Gnostics used Matt. 7:7 as their warrant: "Seek, and you will find." For Christians, Tertullian maintains, the search has ended; the true faith has been found and must only be defended against its erosion by illicit curiosity. For both Irenaeus and Tertullian, illicit curiosity is the true danger of a Gnostic hermeneutics of inquiry.

THE THIRD AND FOURTH CENTURIES

Alexandrian Hermeneutics

The protest of the late-second-century fathers, however, could not stem the tide of the times. Professional, scientific hermeneutics was the wave of the future. The patristic scene in the third and fourth centuries followed the pace set by Christian schools in the centers of Hellenistic culture. One of the oldest school traditions developed in Alexandria. Eusebius speaks of a catechetical school with a succession of famous teachers, beginning with Pantaenus (late second century), Clement of Alexandria, and Origen (*Church History* V.10; VI.6ff.). The impact of these theologians on subsequent Christian history cannot be doubted.

Clement of Alexandria

For Clement, who died before 215, the interpretation of the Jewish Scriptures as a Christian book was only part of a broader hermeneutical challenge. For him, all truth everywhere was identical with Christianity, the final revelation of the Logos of God. But it had to be wrested from the texts by hard work. "All theologians, barbarians and Greeks, hid the beginnings of things and delivered the truth in enigmas and symbols, allego-

15

ries and metaphors and similar figures" (*Stromata* V.21.4). The same was true of the inspired Septuagint and the early Christian writings: "Almost the whole of Scripture is expressed in enigmas" (*Stromata* VI.124.5–6). It was the task of the interpreter who had received the deeper knowledge (*gnōsis*) imparted by Christ to his apostles after the resurrection, to open up the symbolic truth of biblical language to those capable of understanding. Following Philo, Clement freely allegorized the Old Testament. His hermeneutical principle in identifying true meaning was an eclectic mixture of Hellenistic cosmology, soteriology, and morality, combined with the conviction that in the Logos-Christ all adumbrations of truth had found their goal. Thus the words of Jesus and the New Testament writings that Clement used along with other early Christian books did not need much allegorical treatment; their mysteries, pointing to the church and to the life to come, were readily understood by the true Gnostic. Irenaeus and Tertullian probably would have regarded Clement as one of their Gnostic antagonists. In his emphasis on the church, its creed, and its ethics for simple as well as for advanced believers, however, Clement distinguished himself from speculative Gnosticism.

Origen

In Origen (ca. 185–253/54) we encounter one of the great minds and probably the most influential theologian of the early Christian era. Many of his writings are lost due to a later condemnation by the emperor Justinian I in 543. Nevertheless, modern scholarship has been able to piece together large portions of his staggering literary output. Most of it is concerned with biblical interpretation. Origen laid a solid foundation by careful work on the biblical text including its textual history. His *Hexapla*, a comparative text of the Old Testament written in six parallel columns, was still admired by Jerome in Caesarea in the fifth century before it perished during the storms of the Arab conquest. Jerome classified Origen's exegetical writings in three categories: scholia, that is, short explanatory glosses; commentaries; homilies (*Patrologia Latina* 25, 585–86). Most books of the Bible are dealt with in one form or another. Origen also authored the first technical treatise on Christian hermeneutical theory (see chapter V). It forms Book IV of his systematic treatise *On First Principles* and was written between 220 and 230. Much of the original Greek text is preserved in the *Philocalia*, an anthology culled from his writings by Basil of Caesarea and Gregory of Nazianzus around A.D. 358. For the later sections, however, we have to rely on hypothetical reconstruction using Rufinus's Latin translation (ca. 400) and fragments quoted by Jerome. The new translation in this volume follows in general the reconstruction by Görgemanns and Karpp.

The treatise had an apologetic purpose. Origen regarded the Christian Bible as intended by God for the benefit of all serious readers everywhere. Thus, his treatment started out by proving the Scriptures' divine inspiration. The missionary success of the Christian movement, the astonishing fulfillment of prophecy, and the personal experience of every reader with the sacred text provided the evidence. But inspired Scriptures must have a spiritual purpose. Against naive literalists and Marcionites, Origen argued that a simplistic or anthropomorphic understanding was an insult to the divine character of the writings; it exposed God to ridicule. When he finally developed his own theory of biblical interpretation he was careful to start from within. Texts such as Prov. 22:20–21 and *The Shepherd of Hermas, Vision* II.4.3, he argued, suggest a threefold sense of Scripture in analogy to the tripartite anthropology of the philosophers and of Paul: just as human beings consist of body, soul, and spirit, so Scripture edifies by a literal, a moral, and a spiritual sense (II.4). All biblical texts have a spiritual sense; not all have a literal sense as well, even though the large majority do (III.4–5). Origen understood this spiritual sense to refer to the fate of human souls who have their true home in the Platonic realm of "intelligibles," the world of spiritual realities, compared with which the physical world is but a shadow or a material deformation. Thus the letter of the Old Testament stories about Israel and the nations as well as many words of Jesus or Paul must be read as "really" speaking about human souls and their ascent (III.6ff.). Origen found the invitation to formulate rules consonant with these principles in the "stumbling blocks" which the divine author placed before the reader: logical difficulties, impossibilities, apparent untruths, fictitious historical events (III.9). Origen encountered them everywhere, in the narratives as well as in the legal prescriptions, even in the New Testament (III.1–3). Problems of this kind pointed to the need for a deeper understanding which the interpreter must reach by giving careful attention to context, wording, and parallels. And yet, no scrutiny could ever exhaust the depth of wisdom contained in Scripture (III.14). For Scripture is a means to an end, a guide for the soul on its way upward. In this sense, the place of Origen's hermeneutics at the end of his systematic theology is an accurate expression of his underlying principle: Biblical hermeneutics presents the method for *anagōgē*, the ascent of the soul, which is at the heart of his soteriology.

Later Alexandrian Exegetes

Origen's biblical writings had an immense impact on later theology. While his own commentaries did not strictly follow the theory of a threefold sense, his understanding of *anagōgē* as the movement upward from the bodily level to a spiritual sense gave a firm rationale to Christian allegorization. Searching the biblical texts for clues to their higher spiritual meaning became the normative task of the Christian exegete, and with this task came the appropriation of the full arsenal of Hellenistic allegorical techniques: the philological study of words and phrases, etymology, numerology, figuration, natural symbolism, etc. One may deplore the "loss of spontaneity" (J. Daniélou) which this new emphasis entailed. Nevertheless, Origen paved the road for Christian hermeneutics as a professional and scientific enterprise fully in tune with the scholarly standards of his time. This was no small achievement. His successors built upon the foundations which he had laid: Eusebius of Caesarea who expressly denied that Moses and the prophets spoke for their own time at all; Didymus the Blind (313–98) whose prolific exegetical work in the Origenistic tradition has in recent decades become better known through the papyrus find in Toura in Egypt; and Gregory of Nyssa (ca. 335–94), whose *Life of Moses* presents an example of an anagogical or mystical reading of biblical texts in its purest form.

Allegorical Lists

The curious list of allegorical equivalents found in the Greek Papyrus Inv. 3718 of the University of Michigan (see chapter VI) fits into the stream of the Alexandrian tradition. Experts have dated the fragments in the seventh century A.D. on paleographical grounds. The contents, however, reflect longstanding school tradition. Lists of this kind may have been in the hands of preachers or teachers. The choice of texts (Gospels and Proverbs) is puzzling. However, Justin Martyr already allegorized parables of Jesus and extracted christological types from Wisdom books. Moreover, the listing of allegorical equivalents was probably part of the early school tradition of Homeric interpretation. Metrodoros of Lampsakos and the school of Anaxagoras in the fifth century B.C. apparently allegorized Homer's gods and heros in this way: Zeus = Mind; Athena = Art; Agamemnon = Ether; Achilleus = Sun; Helena = Earth, etc. Similar allegorical keys appear in Philo's works and even in the interpretations of Jesus' parables (Matt. 13:18–23, 37–39). The Michigan Papyrus together with parts of the Pseudo-Athanasian *Questions on the New Testament* (in *Patrologia Graeca* 28, 711–15) provides proof that such lists also existed as a literary genre.

Antiochene Hermeneutics

It was precisely against this form of universal mechanical allegory that the rival school of Antioch reacted. The Antiochene church had played an important role in early Christian history and could boast an influential school tradition. The school's early phase was connected with the name of the text critic Lucian (late third century), the admired teacher of Arius and his friends. Its golden age came with the exegete Diodore of Tarsus who died before 394 and the generation of his pupils, Theodore of Mopsuestia, John Chrysostom, and Theodoret of Cyrrhus. Under constant suspicion because of its connection with the

Nestorian heresy, the school's remnant later moved east to Edessa and finally to Nisibis in Persia outside the borders of the empire where exegetical work flourished long into the centuries of Muslim domination (Paul of Nisibis, Babai the Great, Isho'dad of Merv).

The Polemical Scope

There can be little doubt that the hermeneutical theories of the Antiochene school were aimed at the excesses of Alexandrian spiritualism. Careful textual criticism, philological and historical studies, and the cultivation of classical rhetoric had been the hallmark of the pagan schools in the city. Christian exegetes followed in the same path. Modern biblical scholars have sometimes praised the sober attention given to the literal sense by the Antiochene exegetes as a model for today. Alexandrian allegorism, it is claimed, regarded the text of the Bible as a mere springboard for uncontrolled speculation while the Antiochene interpretation took the historical substance seriously and thus was closer to early Christian typology. Indeed, for many Christian scholars typology remains a legitimate hermeneutical device while allegory is classified as an illegitimate distortion. This picture conforms closely to the polemical vision of the Antiochene exegetes themselves. It must be pointed out, however, that the sharp antithesis is a construct. Origen, as we saw, did not deny the historical referent of most texts, and the Antiochene theologians admitted a higher sense of Scriptures which they called *theōria*, a term used by Plato but now turned into a weapon against Alexandrian allegorism. Diodore wrote a treatise, now lost, *On the Difference Between Theōria and Allegoria*, and numerous Antiochene texts spell out the polemic. Yet, at close inspection both allegory and *theōria* speak about the same anagogical dynamic Origen so eloquently described: the biblical text leads the reader upward into spiritual truths that are not immediately obvious and that provide a fuller understanding of God's economy of salvation.

The difference between Alexandria and Antioch seems to reflect more the methodological emphases and priorities of the schools than soteriological principles. In Antioch, the Hellenistic rhetorical tradition, and therefore the rational analysis of biblical language, was stressed more than the philosophical tradition and its analysis of spiritual reality. Moreover, in Alexandria, history was subordinated to a higher meaning; the historical referent of the literal level took second place to the spiritual teaching intended by the divine author. In Antioch, the higher *theōria* remained subject to the foundational *historia,* the faithful (or sometimes even fictional) account of events; deeper truth for the guidance of the soul took second place to the scholarly interest in reconstructing human history and understanding the human language of the inspired writers.

Diodore of Tarsus

Both Diodore of Tarsus and Theodore of Mopsuestia wrote commentaries on the Book of Psalms. Despite some lingering doubts, it seems likely that large portions of Diodore's work are preserved in an eleventh-century manuscript under the name of Anastasius of Nicaea. Both the Prologue to the Psalter and the Preface to Psalm 118 (Psalm 119 of the Masoretic text) contain important hermeneutical reflections (see chapters VII and VIII). The Antiochene polemic against allegorism is expressed here in almost classical formulations. In the eyes of Diodore, allegory was foolishness; it introduced silly fables in the place of the text. Allegorizers abolish history and make one thing mean another. Diodore also explains the Antiochene *theōria:* It is a higher sense, an anagogy, but it adds its spiritual vision to the plain, literal meaning without abrogating history. Thus, it strikes a balance between pagan Hellenistic allegory and un-Christian Jewish literalism. *Theōria* is not identical with a simplistic typology of promise and fulfillment either. In fact, the terminology of type and antitype is missing in Diodore. Rather, the psalms adapt themselves to all kinds of conditions and times. They are truly prophetic, conforming first to their original historical setting but then in an even deeper sense to subsequent situations down to the final resurrection of the dead. While Diodore insists upon the factuality of the original setting and scrutinizes the text for clues to its reconstruction, he also understands Scripture as speaking on a deeper level. The Psalms teach ethics and doctrine; they refute those who deny providence and lend words to the prayers of the afflicted. Their conceptual content may indeed be lifted up into higher anagogy but such *theōria* must be left to those endowed with a "fuller charisma." In short: history is not opposed to *theōria*.

Theodore of Mopsuestia

One major difficulty for the Antiochene polemic was Paul's use of the term *allēgoroumena* in Gal. 4:24 in connection with the story of Sarah and Hagar. It seemed to endorse the Alexandrian practice. Diodore discussed the instance briefly in both texts. We have also a detailed exposition in Theodore's *Commentary on Galatians* (see chapter IX) which, like all of his Pauline commentaries, is preserved in a somewhat rough Latin version of the fifth century. The main argument is that by "allegory" Paul meant the Antiochene *theōria*. Paul knew the Hellenistic term but not the Hellenistic application which would treat the texts like dreams in the night; he gave history priority over all other considerations. His method was to use the actual events behind the historical narrative and to apply them rhetorically to his own situation. For this purpose he even could add features of his own invention such as the "persecution" of Isaac by Ishmael. But his method was based on a comparison which could not point out similarities if the events compared were not real.

Lasting Concerns

Despite Theodore's ingenious effort to dissociate *theōria* from allegory, the difference is not as clear as one might wish. To rescue the *historia* of the biblical story, especially a foundational text like the creation account, from dissolution into uncontrolled speculation may be a laudable intention. But the Alexandrian insistence on a rational critique of anthropomorphic and mythical language as pointing to more than mere history is equally valid. The fact remains that in acknowledging the divine author of Scripture both sides sought deeper meaning and hidden treasures of revelation in the sacred text. The difference lay in the scope of this revelation. The anagogy of Alexandrian *allēgoria* led the soul into a realm of true knowledge where the vision of intelligible truth would crown the road to salvation. The anagogy of Antiochene *theōria,* while conveying glimpses of the one God of All, led humans into a truly moral life which would continue into eternity as an existence free of sin.

THE EARLY WEST

North African Roots

Eclecticism

The Latin writers of the fourth century did not take sides in the hermeneutical dispute between Alexandria and Antioch. Latin hermeneutics went its own way and remained rather conservative. In fact, the new direction initiated by Origen in the third century found a positive echo in the West only a century later. By that time, in the middle of the fourth century, a considerable eclecticism dominated the scene. The writings of both schools started circulating in Latin translations and exerted their influence (initially Philo, Clement of Alexandria, and Origen; later Theodore, John Chrysostom, and others). Soon exegetical handbooks in both traditions were available. Alexandrian allegorism was advocated in the *Treatise on Mysteries* by Hilary of Poitiers (ca. 315–67), the first exposition of Origenistic hermeneutics by a Western writer, and Eucherius of Lyon's *Formulae Spiritalis Intelligentiae* (ca. 450). Antiochene hermeneutics colored much of Jerome's exegetical work. Its emphases were kept alive by such manuals as Junilius Africanus's Latin version of a school text on biblical rhetoric written by Paul of Nisibis (ca. 542) or by the *Introduction to the Holy Scriptures* from the pen of a monk, Hadrian, in the fifth century. Cassiodorus the senator (ca. 485–580) mentions these together with Tyconius and Augustine as standard literature in biblical hermeneutics (*Institutiones* I.10).

Tertullian's Common-sense Approach

Augustine's magisterial treatise on biblical hermeneutics, *On Christian Doctrine* (396/97; finished in 427), did not hint at a

23

controversy over allegorism. In a way it reflected the interests of both sides. It stressed, on the one hand, the spiritual goal of building up the dual love of God and neighbor; but it also insisted upon the full use of grammatical, historical, and linguistic knowledge in the service of biblical interpretation. Even Augustine's own figurative exegesis, however, did not clear up the chaos of Christian hermeneutical terminology. Early on he borrowed heavily from a rhetorical tradition in which Cicero occupied a place of honor. The first Latin Christian writer, Tertullian, had been a legally trained rhetorician thoroughly familiar with Cicero's methods of persuasion, which he employed with great skill. The same Tertullian, however, hesitated to apply the rules of rhetorical figuration to the analysis of biblical texts. Even the prophets, he cautioned, said many things without allegory or figure; not everything in the Bible comes as image, shadow, or parable (*On the Resurrection* 19–21). Like Irenaeus, Tertullian used allegory to illumine the typical sense of the Old Testament, drawing on the themes of the early Christian tradition, but he exercised even greater restraint. The biblical text had first of all a natural meaning which normally culminated in a moral message. Even the dietary and ritual laws of the Old Testament did not hide deep secrets but were given to promote self-control and curb idolatry among the Jews (*Against Marcion* II.18.2–3). The background of this common-sense hermeneutics was Tertullian's struggle against Jews, Marcionites, and Gnostics. It was a sign of heresy to find allegories, parables, and enigmas everywhere (*Scorpiace* 11.4). The answer to such speculative interpretations was not to be found in new hermeneutical rules but in strict adherence to the Rule of Faith.

Cyprian and the Testimonia Tradition

The reluctance to engage in speculative allegorization, the preference given to traditional typology, and an eclectic use of hermeneutical rules remained characteristic of the Western development. This was true especially of North Africa where pastoral and catechetical concerns rather than the teachings of schools determined theological emphases. Cyprian, bishop of

Carthage during the persecutions of 250–58, may illustrate the point. His writings were steeped in the language of the Bible which he knew in an African Latin version. For him, it is not so much the divine Logos but the Spirit that speaks in the Scriptures, welding together the books of the Old and New Testament into a single revelation of God's plan of salvation. Cyprian's thinking still moved in the framework of the types, figures, and images which were so characteristic of early Christian apologetics. Among his works we find the best-known examples of *testimonia* books, a literary genre in which Old Testament verses and passages are arranged under topical headings to prove or illustrate main tenets of the Christian faith. Biblical scholars have debated the possibility of very early Christian *testimonia* sources for a long time. Despite the discovery of a leaf with messianic texts at Qumran (*4Q Test.*), however, attempts at identifying a *testimonia* book behind the Old Testament quotations in the New Testament (J. Rendel Harris) have not led to satisfactory results. Recent scholars (C.H. Dodd; J. Daniélou) stress the dynamic growth of the *testimonia* tradition in all its forms of transmission, oral and written. In North Africa, part of the earlier *testimonia* tradition probably was shaped by anti-Jewish polemics as several treatises *Against the Jews* reveal (Tertullian; Pseudo-Cyprian), another part by the catechetical interest in messianic proof texts. Cyprian apparently organized these traditions and expanded them. His *Testimonia ad Quirinum* group them in three categories: Against the Jews, messianic prophecies, Christian virtues. Another treatise of the same genre, *Ad Fortunatum,* represents his personal selection of biblical texts suited for the encouragement of Christians at a time of impending persecution.

Tyconius the Donatist

Augustine's Judgment on Tyconius

The North African situation of a century later is reflected in Tyconius's *Book of Rules* (ca. 380), the first hermeneutical treatise written in the Latin West (see chapter X). Although he remained attached to the schismatic Donatist church throughout his life, Tyconius commanded considerable respect among his contemporaries as a theologian and exegete. His *Commentary on the Revelation of John,* known today in fragmentary form only, dominated the Western interpretation of this biblical book for centuries with its shift from a traditional millennarian reading (Tertullian, Hippolytus, Victorinus of Pettau) to a moral-symbolic understanding with broad implications for all times. It seems that Augustine shared the general respect (cf. *Retractations* II.18; *Epistle 249 to Restitutus*); his eschatology, ecclesiology, soteriology, and hermeneutics probably were more deeply influenced by Tyconius than one might notice at first glance. In his manual, *On Christian Doctrine,* Augustine included something like a critical book review of Tyconius's *Book of Rules* (III.xxx– xxxvi.42–56). He quoted the Prologue but disagreed with the claim that these rules would solve "all obscurities" in the Law; he then proceeded to a detailed summary of each of the seven rules themselves. The second and the third rules, according to Augustine, were wrongly labeled; the second should have been called "On the true and the mixed Body of the Lord," and the third was not a "rule" clarifying obscurities but a theological treatise on the topics Augustine himself had discussed in *The Spirit and the Letter.* Apart from these minor points and a warning about the Donatist point of view, however, Augustine's endorsement was complete and enthusiastic. A critical edition of Tyconius's Latin text has been available since 1884, but all too often Augustine's review serves as a substitute for a close study of the *Book of Rules* itself. Due to limitations of space, our translation presents the first three Rules only. We have added new section numbers which are not found in the editions.

Hermeneutical Principles

Tyconius stood squarely in the tradition of North African hermeneutics. He shared its store of *testimonia,* its emphasis on the unity of Old and New Testament history, and its interest in applying the biblical message to the contemporary situation. For him, as for Cyprian, Scripture was first and foremost prophecy, not only of Christ's first advent, but of his continuous coming in his body and at his final advent. In fact, Scripture "describes nothing else but the church." Tyconius's hermeneutics, therefore, starts with the principle that all exegesis has an ecclesiological goal: The Bible illustrates and interprets the struggles of the contemporary church. Scholars are not agreed on whether he combined this interest with an imminent expectation of the end of the world or was thinking more generally of the "true" church, exemplified by the Donatists of the late fourth century, expecting in the midst of persecution some kind of public vindication against the "false" church, the majority, which is always the body of the devil. His thoroughly symbolic interpretation of the *Apocalypse of John* would point in the latter direction. But even if his own use of apocalyptic language implied an expectation of the impending end, his hermeneutical concentration on the situation of the church militant between the ages was the feature that appealed to Augustine and the generations after him.

Hermeneutical Rules

Tyconius's Rules approach the task by giving careful attention to the peculiarities of biblical language. The texts themselves offer the clue to their ecclesiological meaning. Tyconius starts with the observation that the wording of biblical passages often shows rhetorical patterns which point to several subjects governing a single sentence or to a transition from one subject to another in the same verse. Reason alone, that is, grammatical and logical analysis, must discern these subtle shifts and apply them to the intended distinctions between the Lord and the Body, the whole body and a part, or evil and good parts within the same body. Rule three unfolds the last point by a sophisticated rehearsal of the Pauline dialectic of law and promise, discussing all the pertinent texts: Abraham's seed which received the promise was twofold already in Isaac and Ishmael, Jacob and Esau; the true church is always two people in one because its members, the true heirs, grasp the promise of righteousness by their faith precisely under the threat of the Law. In the one body composed of the children of Abraham the Law holds sway over the carnal part, the children of the devil, from whom the true church must depart, revealing the false brethren in their real identity. This vision of history as the battleground of the true and the false church found its lasting expression in Augustine's two cities characterized by the two loves of God and the world. Augustine's hermeneutics was a commentary on this Tyconian theme: The goal of all biblical interpretation must be the double love of God and neighbor, the ordering of the Christian life toward our heavenly home (*On Christian Doctrine* I.xxxv–xxxvi.39–40).

The Fourfold Sense of Scripture

Western hermeneutics in the Augustinian tradition finally crystallized its rules into the standard form of a fourfold sense of Scripture—literal, allegorical, tropological (moral), and anagogical. Augustine himself had worked with a different list for the Old Testament, based on the Greek technical terms of a rhetorical analysis of language: history, aetiology, analogy, and allegory (*On the Usefulness of Belief* III.5–9). But the technical focus on language analysis was not enough; the fourfold sense needed to express a hermeneutical principle. The standard form appeared first in a passage of John Cassian's *Conferences* XIV.8 (ca. 420) which also introduced the standard example of Jerusalem: literally, Jerusalem means the city of the Jews; allegorically, the church (Ps. 46:4–5); tropologically, the soul (Ps. 147:1–2, 12); anagogically, our heavenly home (Gal. 4:26). Cassian's explanation, which drew heavily on Origen's hermeneutical theory, made it plain that the fourfold sense was never a mechanical set of rules which professional exegetes would have to apply to every passage of Scripture. Rather, in the framework of the Western hermeneutical focus on the life of the church, they offered an ingenious synthesis of all the main strands of patristic hermeneutics to be handed down to the Latin Middle Ages. The attention to be given to the literal sense preserved the grammatical and historical emphases of the Antiochene school; the allegorical sense expressed the typological understanding of the Old Testament and its rich early Christian tradition; the tropological sense allowed for the interests of Jewish and Christian moralists from the rabbis and Philo to Tertullian and Chrysostom; the anagogical sense kept alive the central concern of Alexandrian exegesis for a spiritual reading of Scriptures.

The translations in this volume have been made from the best critical editions of the Hebrew, Greek, and Latin texts as listed in the first part of the bibliography. Whenever possible, biblical quotations have been identified and adapted from standard modern translations; they have been newly translated, however, when the patristic source followed the Septuagint or an Old Latin version. The reader will notice that almost everywhere the numbering of the Psalms follows that of the Septuagint, which is one count off from that of the Hebrew Bible after Psalm 9. Thus, a verse quoted as Ps. 46:4 in this volume would be Ps. 47:4 in most English Bibles.

II.

Sifra

THE EXEGETICAL RULES (*MIDDÔT*) OF RABBI ISHMAEL AND RABBI HILLEL

A Tradition of Rabbi Ishmael

Rabbi Ishmael said: The *torâ* is expounded by thirteen rules:

1. Light and heavy [*qal wāḥōmer;* conclusion from the less important to the more important and vice versa];
2. Equal ordinance [*gĕzērâ šāwâ;* verbal analogy];
3. Building a family [*binyān 'āb;* generalization] from one passage;
4. Building a family from two passages;
5. General and specific [*kelāl ûpĕrāt*]; specific and general;
6. General and specific, and again general. In this case one can only conclude something which agrees with the specific;
7. General which needs the specific, and specific which needs the general;
8. Anything contained in a general statement and singled out in order to make a specific point is not singled out in order to make this point for its own sake alone, but for the general statement in its entirety;
9. Anything contained in a general statement and singled out in order to impose a new requirement still in line with the subject matter of the general statement is singled out in order to ease (the burden), not to make it heavier;
10. Anything contained in a general statement and singled out in order to impose a new requirement not in line with the

subject matter of the general statement is singled out either to ease (the burden) or to make it heavier;

11. With regard to anything contained in a general statement and singled out in order to establish a norm for a new subject, one must not apply it back to the general statement unless Scripture explicitly places it there;
12. Something learned from the context [*mē'inyānô*], and something learned from that which follows;
13. In the same way, two passages which contradict each other until a third comes and adjudicates between them.

1. *Light and heavy.* How (does this rule work)? "And the Lord said to Moses: If her father had but spit in her face, should she not be shamed seven days?" [Num. 12:14]. (Using the rule of) light and heavy: In the case of the deity, (it should be) fourteen days. It is sufficient, however, for the result of an inference to be equivalent to the law from which the inference is drawn: "So Miriam was shut up outside the camp seven days and then was brought in again" [ibid.].

2. *Equal ordinance.* How (does this rule work)? Scripture says with reference to the paid keeper: "(An oath by the Lord shall be between them both to see whether) he has not put his hand to his neighbor's property" [Exod. 22:8]. As a man clears the heirs of liability in the case of a paid keeper about whom it is said: "He has not put his hand (to his neighbor's property)," he shall also clear the heirs of liability in the case of an unpaid keeper about whom it is said: "He has not put his hand (to his neighbor's property)."

3. *Building a family from one passage.* How (does this rule work)? What is applicable to the bed (of an unclean person) is not applicable to his seat and vice versa. But the two, bed and seat, are equal in one respect: they are both conveniences on which humans are meant to rest. A male with a (gonorrheal) discharge makes them unclean through (lying or sitting on them with) his larger part so that they render people unclean if they are touched or carried, and through clothing. Thus, the same rule applies to everything made for human rest alone: A male with a discharge will make it unclean by his larger part so that it

renders people unclean if they touch or carry it, and through clothing. An exception is the wagon seat because it is also designed for a different kind of carrying.

4. *Building a family from two passages.* How (does this rule work)? The provision about the lamps [Lev. 24:1–4] is not applicable to the passage about putting the unclean out of the camp [Num. 5:1–4] and vice versa. But they have in common the word "Command!" It is valid (in both cases) for the immediate situation as well as for all time to come [because of Lev. 24:2].

5. *General and specific.* How (does this rule work)? "If a man delivers to his neighbor an ass or an ox or a sheep": this is the specific; "or any beast to keep": this is the general [Exod. 22:10]. *Specific and general.* The general appears as an addition to the specific.

6. *General and specific, and again general.* How (does this rule work)? "And spend your money for whatever you desire": this is the general; "oxen, or sheep, or wine, or strong drink": this is the specific; "Whatever your appetite craves": this is the general again [Deut. 14:26]. In the case of general and specific and again general one may derive only what agrees with the specific. That is to say: If the specific is clearly defined as a product of the fruits of the earth, then I (the Lord) can only accept that which is a product of the fruits of the earth.

7. *General which needs the specific, and specific which needs the general.* How (does this rule work)? "Consecrate to me all the firstborn" [Exod. 13:2]. One could think that this is to be understood to include the female. Therefore, it states [in v. 12]: "all the firstborn that are male." If male, one could think this applies even if a female has left the womb before him. Therefore it states: "(firstborn males) opening the womb." If it speaks of males opening the womb, one could think this applies even if another fetus extracted by caesarean section preceded him. Therefore it says: "first*born*." This is a case of general which needs the specific and specific which needs the general.

8. *Anything contained in a general statement and singled out in order to make a specific point is not singled out in order to make this point for its own sake alone, but for the general statement in its entirety.* How (does this rule work)? "But the

person who eats of the flesh of the sacrifice of the Lord's peace offering while an uncleanness is upon him, that person shall be cut off" [Lev. 7:20]. Now peace offerings are included in the general category of all sacrifices. As it is written: "This is the law of the burnt offering, of the cereal offering, of the sin offering, of the guilt offering, of the consecration, and of the peace offerings" [Lev. 7:37]. When, however, something is deduced from the general in order to make a specific point, it is not deduced in order to make this point just for its own sake but in order to teach something about the general in its entirety. Thus, peace offerings are specially mentioned among sacrifices whose sanctity is the sanctity of the altar. Therefore, I (the Lord) only accept all those things whose sanctity is the sanctity of the altar. An exception are the offerings for the repair of the Temple.

9. *Anything contained in a general statement and singled out in order to impose a new requirement still in line with the subject matter of the general statement is singled out in order to ease (the burden), not to make it heavier.* How (does this rule work)? "But when there is in the skin of one's body a boil that has healed" [Lev. 13:18]. It is also written: "Or when the body has a burn on its skin" [v. 24]. But are not the boil and the burn included in the general category of all leprous sores? (Our rule states that) if they have been singled out from the general category in order to impose a new requirement which is still in line with its subject matter, they have been singled out in order to ease (the burden), not to make it heavier. Thus, these two have been singled out in order to ease the burden of such (victims) so that they are not judged according to the rules concerning wild growth of flesh but are judged to need only one more week (of isolation).

10. *Anything contained in a general statement and singled out in order to impose a new requirement not in line with the subject matter of the general statement is singled out either to ease (the burden) or to make it heavier.* How (does this rule work)? "When a man or a woman has a sore on the head or the chin" [Lev. 13:29]. But are not head and chin included in the general category of skin and flesh? (Our rule states that) if they have been singled out in order to impose a new requirement not

in line (with the general statement), they have been singled out either to ease (the burden) or to make it heavier. Thus, these two have been singled out in order to ease the burden for such (victims) inasmuch as they are not judged by the rules concerning white hair [Lev. 13:10,20,25], but also to make it heavier for them inasmuch as they are judged by the rules concerning yellow hair [Lev. 13:30–37].

11. *With regard to anything contained in a general statement and singled out in order to establish a norm for a new subject, one must not apply it back to the general statement unless Scripture explicitly places it there.* How (does this rule work)? "He shall kill the lamb in the place where they kill the sin offering and the burnt offering, in the holy place" [Lev. 14:13]. There is no need to continue by saying: "For the guilt offering, like the sin offering, belongs to the priest" [ibid.]. Since, however, the guilt offering is singled out in order to establish a norm for new subject matter, namely, (the smearing of blood) on the thumb of the right hand and the big toe of the right foot and the right earlobe, one could assume that it does not require a sprinkling of blood on the altar. Therefore the text reads: "For the guilt offering like the sin offering belongs to the priest." Note that Scripture explicitly applies it back to the general statement in order to make clear that, just as the sin offering requires a sprinkling on the altar, so the guilt offering requires a sprinkling on the altar also.

12. *Something learned from the context.* How (does this rule work)? "If a man's hair has fallen from his head he is bald but he is clean" [Lev. 13:40]. One could think he is free from all uncleanness. Therefore it says: "But if there is on the bald head behind or on the bald forehead a reddish-white diseased spot" [Lev. 13:42]. The thing learned from the context is that he is not free from every uncleanness but only from that of scurfs.

Something learned from that which follows. How (does this rule work)? "When I put a leprous disease in a house in the land of your possession" [Lev. 14:34]. The ordinary sense is: (By a fungous infection) a house which contains stones, timber, and plaster is made unclean. One could think that (such an infection) also renders unclean a house which contains no stones,

timber, and plaster. Therefore it says "He shall break down the house, its stones, its timber, and all its plaster" [v. 35]. The thing learned from that which follows is that a house is not made unclean unless it contains stones, timber, and plaster.
   13. *Two passages which contradict each other until a third comes and adjudicates between them.* How (does this rule work)? One passage reads: "And the Lord came down on Mount Sinai, to the top of the mountain" [Exod. 19:20]. But another passage reads: "Out of heaven he let you hear his voice that he might discipline you" [Deut. 4:36]. The third passage decides: "(You have seen for yourselves) that I have talked with you from heaven" [Exod. 20:22]. It teaches that the Holy One, blessed be He, bowed the heaven of the highest heaven down to Mount Sinai and spoke to them. David says this in the book of Psalms: "And he bowed the heavens and came down, and darkness was under his feet" [Ps. 18:10].

(A Tradition of Rabbi Hillel)

Hillel the Elder expounded seven rules before the Elders of Bathîra:

1. Light and heavy [*qal wāḥōmer*]
2. Equal ordinance [*gĕzērâ šāwâ*]
3. Building a family [*binyān 'āb*]
4. Two passages [*šĕnê kĕtûbîm*]
5. General and specific [*kelāl ûpĕrāt*]
6. Deduction from another passage [*kāyôṣê' bô bĕmāqôm 'aḥēr*]
7. Something learned from the context [*dābār hallāmēd mē 'inyānô*]

   One passage reads: "And when Moses went into the tent of meeting to speak with the Lord" [Num. 7:89]. But another passage reads: "And Moses was not able to enter the tent of meeting" [Exod. 40:35]. The decision is made by the words: "because the cloud abode upon it" [ibid.]. Learn from this, therefore, that every time the cloud was there Moses did not enter. When the cloud moved away, he entered and spoke with

Him. Rabbi José the Galilean said: "Behold, it is written: And the priests could not stand to minister because of the cloud, for the glory of the Lord filled the house of the Lord [1 Kings 8:11]. This text teaches that permission to injure was given to the angels. A Scripture verse says this also: I will cover you with my hand until I have passed by [Exod. 33:22]. It teaches that permission to injure was given to the angels. And another Scripture verse says it also: Therefore I swore in my anger that they should not enter my rest [Ps. 95:11]. When my anger subsides they will enter my rest."

III.

Ptolemy

LETTER TO FLORA

(Epiphanius, *Panarion* 33)

(III,1) My fair sister Flora, few people before our time have understood the law ordained through Moses due to their lack of accurate knowledge concerning the one who ordained it as well as its precepts. I believe this will be clear to you as well once you have been instructed concerning the contradictory opinions people hold about it. (2) For some say that it was laid down as law by God the Father. Others, however, leaning in the opposite direction, insist that it was ordained by the adversary, the destructive devil, to whom they also attribute the creation of the world, affirming that he is the father and maker of this universe. (3) Both sides are completely wrong. They disagree with each other and have missed, each in its own way, the truth of the matter at hand. (4) Plainly, the law was not ordained by the perfect God and Father. It is secondary, not only being imperfect and in need of completion by someone else, but also containing precepts which are not in harmony with the nature and intention of such a God. (5) On the other hand, attributing a law which prohibits injustice to the injustice of the adversary is the mistake of people who do not heed the words of the Savior. "A house or a city divided against itself cannot stand," explained our Savior [Matt. 12:25]. (6) Furthermore, the apostle states that the creation of the world is the Savior's work: "All things were made through him, and without him nothing was made" [John 1:3]; thus he demolished in advance the unfounded wisdom of those falsifiers and declared that the world is the work of a God

37

who is just and hates evil, not of a God who destroys. Those false teachings are shared only by thoughtless people who do not take into account the providence of the creator, people whose sight is impaired in regard not only to the eye of the soul but even the eye of the body [cf. Matt. 13:13–15].

(7) From my above remarks it will be clear to you how these people have missed the truth, each of the two sides in its own way. One side does not know the God of justice, the other does not know the Father of All who was revealed by the only one who came and knew him [cf. John 1:18; Matt. 11:27]. (8) It remains for us who have been deemed worthy of the knowledge of both of these to explain to you and describe in detail the law itself, its nature, and the one who ordained it, the lawgiver. We shall draw the proofs of our statements from the words of our Savior, which alone can lead us without stumbling to the comprehension of that which is.

(IV,1) Now the first thing to be learned is that the entire law encompassed by Moses' Pentateuch was not laid down by a single lawgiver, I mean God alone, but there are also some precepts in it which were ordained by human beings. The words of the Savior teach us that it is divided in three parts: (2) There is God himself and his legislation; then there is Moses, not in the sense that God legislated through Moses but that Moses himself, starting from his own reflections, acted as lawgiver in some instances; and there are finally the elders of the people who, as we find, first introduced some of the precepts on their own. (3) You may learn immediately how the truth of this can be proved by considering the words of the Savior. (4) Somewhere in a discussion with people who debated with him about which kind of divorce the law allowed, the Savior said to them: "Because of your hardness of heart Moses allowed a man to divorce his wife; but this was not so from the beginning" [Matt. 19:8]. For God, so it is written, joined these two into one couple, "and what God has joined together let no one put asunder," he said [Matt. 19:6]. (5) Here he explains that there is a law of God which prohibits the divorce of a wife from her husband; but there is another law, a law of Moses, which allows this bond between two people to be divorced on account of hardness of heart.

Consequently, Moses is legislating contrary to God, since separating a couple is contrary to not separating a couple. (6) If, however, we proceed to examine Moses' intention in formulating such a law, we find that he did not act of his own will but was forced by necessity on account of the weakness of the people to whom the law was addressed. (7) Since some of them became disgusted with their wives, they were unable to follow through with God's intention that they should not be allowed to dismiss their wives, and they ran the risk of turning even more toward injustice and thus toward their destruction. (8) Therefore Moses, wanting to put an end to this disgust which had left them in danger of perishing, in view of the circumstances replaced a greater evil by a lesser one, so to speak, and gave them the divorce law on his own, as a kind of second law. (9) He thought that, if they could not keep God's law, they might at least keep this one and not turn toward deeds of injustice and evil from which their utter destruction would follow. (10) This was really the intention according to which we find Moses to have introduced legislation contrary to God. At any rate, it remains indisputable that Moses' law is different from the law of God as we have demonstrated here, even though our demonstration was based on only one example. (11) Furthermore, the Savior makes it plain that there are also some traditions of the elders interwoven with the law. These are his words: "For God commanded: Honor your father and your mother that it may go well with you." (12) "You, however, have said," he continues addressing the elders: "The support you should have received from me has been given to God; and thus you have made void the law of God for the sake of your tradition," that is, the tradition of the elders. (13) "Isaiah spoke about this when he said: This people honors me with their lips but their heart is far from me; in vain they worship me, teaching as doctrines the precepts of men" [Matt. 15:6 – 9; Isa. 29:13]. (14) From all of this it is clearly evident that the entire law of which we have been speaking falls into three parts: We find in it the legislation of Moses, the legislation of the elders, and the legislation of God himself. Now this very division of the whole law which we have just laid out brings to light the truth which is in it.

(V, 1) To take things further, the one part which is the law of God himself is again divided into three kinds: First, the pure legislation not entangled with evil; this is called law in the primary sense. The Savior did not come to abolish it but to complete it [Matt. 5:17], for the law he completed was not alien to him but needed completion because it did not possess perfection. Second, the legislation entangled with the inferior and with injustice; this is the part which the Savior abolished because it was incongruous with his nature. (2) The third kind is the typological and symbolical legislation ordained in the image of spiritual and higher things; this is the part which the Savior transferred from the realm of sense perception and appearance to the realm of the spiritual and the invisible. (3) Now God's law in its pure form, unentangled with the inferior, is the Decalogue, those ten words arranged in two tablets to prohibit things one must not do and to enjoin things one must do. Although they present the legislation in a pure form they needed completion by the Savior since they did not possess perfection. (4) The law entangled with injustice is the one which inflicts vengeance and retribution on those who have first committed an injustice. It commands tearing out an eye for an eye, a tooth for a tooth, and avenging murder with murder [Exod. 21:23 – 24; Matt. 5:38]. Now the second person to commit an injustice does no less injustice than the first; the difference lies in the sequence, but the action is the same. (5) Otherwise, this commandment was indeed just, and it still is, inasmuch as it was ordained as a modification of the pure law because of the weakness of those for whom the law was given. It is, however, incongruous with the nature and goodness of the Father of All. (6) Under the circumstances, the commandment was perhaps appropriate; worse than that, it was necessary. For the God who, in saying: "You shall not kill" [Exod. 20:13], does not want even a single murder to be committed, issues a second law and decides on two murders when he commands that the murderer be killed also [cf. Exod. 21:12; Matt. 5:21]. He who had forbidden even the one murder did not notice that he was trapped by necessity. (7) Therefore the Son, coming from him, abolished this part of the law while admitting that it was indeed of God. He counts it as belonging to the old dispensation together with other such passages; he quotes as one of them: "God commanded: He who speaks evil of father or mother, let him surely die" [Exod. 21:17; Matt. 15:4].

(8) Finally, there is the typological part, the one ordained in the image of spiritual and higher things. I am speaking of the part containing legislation about sacrifices, circumcision, the Sabbath, fasting, the Passover, unleavened bread, and the like. (9) All of these were images and symbols, and as such they underwent a transformation when the truth was made manifest. In terms of outward appearance and external performance they were abolished, but in terms of spiritual significance they were lifted up. The words remained, the contents were changed. (10) For the Savior too commanded us to offer up sacrifices, not by means of irrational animals or gifts of incense as had been the case before, but through gifts of spiritual praise, glorification, and thanksgiving, and through sharing and charity toward our neighbors. (11) He also desires that we be circumcised, not in terms of the bodily foreskin but in terms of the spiritual heart. (12) He wants us to keep the Sabbath, for he wishes us to rest from doing evil. He desires us to fast, although he does not want us to engage in physical but in spiritual fasting in which we practice abstinence from all evil. (13) Nevertheless, even among our people the external practice of fasting is being observed; its reasonable exercise can bring some benefit to the soul if it is done not in order to imitate others, nor out of habit, nor out of regard for the special day, as if a particular day was set aside for it. (14) At the same time, it can serve as a reminder of the true fast so that in the external practice those who are still unable to keep the true fast may have a reminder of it. (15) Similarly, the apostle Paul makes clear that the Passover and the unleavened bread were images when he says: "Christ our passover has been sacrificed," and then continues: "in order that you may be unleavened, having no part in the leaven"—by leaven he means here evil—"but may be a new sweet lump" [1 Cor. 5:7].

(VI, 1) Thus even the part which is generally admitted to be God's law falls into three categories: first, the one completed by the Savior, for the commandments, "you shall not kill, you shall not commit adultery, you shall not swear falsely," are included in his prohibition of anger, lust, and swearing [Matt. 5:21 – 37]. (2) The second category is the one which is totally abolished. For the commandment, "an eye for an eye and a tooth for a tooth," entangled as it is with injustice and in itself leading to injustice, was abolished by the Savior through its opposite; (3) opposites cancel each other: "For I say to you: do not in any way resist the one who is evil; but if anyone strikes you, turn to him the other cheek also" [Matt. 5:39]. (4) Finally, there is the category of that which has been transferred and changed from the physical to the spiritual, the symbolic legislation ordained in the image of higher things. (5) For images and symbols pointing to things beyond themselves were valid as long as the truth had not come. Now that the truth is here, however, one must do the works of the truth, not the works of an image. (6) His disciples made this clear, as did the apostle Paul. The latter pointed to the category of images, as we mentioned already, by speaking of the Passover for us and of the unleavened bread. He pointed to the category of the law entangled with injustice by saying: "He abolished the law of commandments and ordinances" [Eph. 2:15]. He pointed, finally, to the category not entangled with anything inferior by stating: "So the law is holy, and the commandment is holy and just and good" [Rom. 7:12].

(VII, 1) As far as I have been able in a few brief words, I think I have sufficiently demonstrated to you the presence of legislation introduced by human authors, as well as the threefold division of the very law of God. (2) It now remains for us to define who this God is who ordained the law. Even this, I think, has been demonstrated to you, if you have listened carefully, by what has already been said. (3) For if the law was not ordained by the perfect God himself, as we have shown, and certainly not by the devil—this must not even be said out loud—then the one who ordained the law is still another one beside them. (4) He is the creator (*dēmiourgos*) and maker of this whole world and of all that is in it. Being different from the essence of the other two and standing in the middle between them he may rightly be given the name, "the Middle." (5) Now, given the fact that the perfect God is good by his very nature—he actually is good, for our Savior declared that one only is the good God, his own

Father whom he revealed [Matt. 19:17]—and the one with the nature of the adversary is bad and evil and characterized by injustice, he who stands in the middle between them and is neither good nor in any way evil or unjust, may be termed "just" in a sense proper only to him since he is the arbitrator of a justice according to his own standards. (6) This God will be inferior to the perfect God and lower than his justice. He is begotten, not unbegotten, for one only is the unbegotten Father from whom all things are [1 Cor. 8:6] because in its proper way everything depends on him. But this God is superior to, and mightier than, the adversary. He is of an essence and nature different from the essence of either of these. (7) The essence of the adversary is corruption and darkness; he is material and multiform. The essence of the unbegotten Father of All, on the other hand, is incorruption and the self-existent, simple, singly formed light [cf. James 1:17]. The essence of the creator (*dēmiourgos*), however, produced a twofold power, yet he himself is the image of the greater God. (8) For the present, do not be troubled because you want to learn how, out of one single principle of everything which we confess and believe to be simple, out of a principle which is unbegotten, incorruptible, and good, these other natures came to be, the nature of corruption and of the Middle, natures constituted by a different essence, when it is in the nature of the good to beget and bring forth that which is similar to it and of the same essence. (9) For if God grants it, you will receive in proper order instruction concerning the principle and the generation of these as well, when you are deemed worthy of the apostolic tradition, which we also have received by succession along with the requirement to prove all our statements through the teaching of our Savior.

(10) I am not tired, my sister Flora, having told you these things in a few words. I had to be concise in what I wrote here, but at the same time sufficient light was shed on the topic under discussion. This will be of enormous benefit to you in your next steps if, having received fertile seeds like a fair and good soil, you show forth the fruit which grows from them [cf. Matt. 13:23].

IV.

Irenaeus

AGAINST HERESIES

(IV.26.1) Therefore, anyone who reads the Scriptures attentively will find in them the word concerning Christ and the prefiguration of the new calling. For Christ is "the treasure hidden in a field" [Matt. 13:44], that is, in the Scriptures which are in the world, for "the field is the world" [Matt. 13:38]; he was hidden, for he was signified by types and parabolic expressions which on the human level could not be understood before the consummation of that which was prophesied had been reached, namely, the coming of Christ. For this reason the prophet Daniel was told: "Block up these words and seal the book until the time of consummation, until many learn and knowledge achieves fullness. For at the time when the dispersion will reach its end, they shall understand all these things" [Dan. 12:4,9–10]. Jeremiah also says: "In the last days they shall understand these things" [Jer. 23:20]. Every prophecy is enigmatic and ambiguous for human minds before it is fulfilled. But when the time has arrived and the prediction has come true, then prophecies find their clear and unambiguous interpretation. This is the reason that the law resembles a fable when it is read by Jews at the present time; for they do not have the explanation of it all, namely, the coming of the Son of God as man. But when it is read by Christians, it is indeed a treasure hidden in the field but revealed and explained by the cross of Christ. It enriches human understanding, shows forth the wisdom of God, reveals God's dispensations concerning the human race, prefigures the kingdom of Christ, and proclaims the inheritance of holy Jerusalem in advance. It announces that a person who loves God will progress even to the point of seeing God and hearing his word, and by listening to this word shall be glorified to such a degree that others will not be able to look upon his glorious face. Daniel expressed it in these words: "Those who understand will shine like the brightness of the firmament and from among the multitude of the righteous like the stars for ever and ever" [Dan. 12:3]. Thus, a person who reads the Scriptures in the manner we have indicated—indeed, the Lord used this kind of discourse with his disciples after his resurrection from the dead, demonstrating to them from the Scriptures that "Christ had to suffer and to enter into his glory, and that remission of sins must be preached in his name throughout all the world" [Luke 24:46–47]—such a person will be a perfect disciple, "like a householder who brings forth from his store things new and old" [Matt. 13:52].

(2) Therefore, one must listen carefully to the presbyters in the church, the ones who have received their succession from the apostles, as we have shown, and who have obtained, together with the succession of the episcopacy, the sure charism of truth according to the good pleasure of the Father. Others, however, who draw back from the original succession and assemble wherever they please, must be looked upon with suspicion; they should be regarded as heretics pursuing perverse ideas, or as schismatics, puffed up and self-pleasing, or again as hypocrites acting as they do for the sake of profit and vainglory.

All of these have strayed from the truth. Now, the heretics who are carrying foreign fire, that is, foreign doctrines, to the altar of God will be consumed by fire from heaven as were Nadab and Abiud [Lev. 10:2]; those who rise up against the truth and counsel others against the church of God will stay in hell, swallowed up by the depth of the earth as was the clan of Korah, Dathan, and Abiram [Num.16:31–32]; those who split and tear apart the unity of the church will receive from God the same punishment as Jeroboam [1 Kings 14:10–11].

(3) But regarding those who are presbyters in the eyes of many yet serve their own passions and fail to give the fear of God first place in their hearts; who are puffed up with the pride of hold-

ing the first place; who do evil in secret and say, "no one sees us" [Dan. 13:20 = Susannah]: they will be convicted by the Word himself who does not judge according to appearance and has no regard for the face, but looks into the heart. And they will hear these words which come from the prophet Daniel: "O you seed of Canaan and not of Judah! Beauty has seduced you and love has perverted your heart. You who have grown old in evil days, now your sins which you have committed for a long time by rendering unjust judgments have come out; you condemned the innocent and freed the guilty although the Lord commands: The innocent and the just you shall not put to death" [Dan. 13:56, 52–53 = Susannah]. The Lord himself said of them: "But if that wicked servant says in his heart: My master delays his coming, and starts beating servants and maids, eating, drinking, and getting drunk, the master of that servant will come on a day he does not know and at an hour he does not anticipate and will cut him in pieces and appoint him his share with the unbelievers" [Matt. 24:48–51].

(4) One must, therefore, stay away from people of this kind altogether. One must cling, as we have said, to those who guard the succession of the apostles and, in concert with the order of the presbyterate, offer sound preaching and irreproachable conduct as an example and for the correction of others. In this way Moses, who was entrusted with such an eminent position of leadership, cleared himself before God by relying on his good conscience: "I have not coveted," he said, "what I received from any of these men, nor have I done evil to any of them" [Num. 16:15]. In the same way, Samuel, who judged the people for so many years and exercised leadership over Israel without a trace of pride, cleared himself at the end and said: "I have lived before you from my youth to this day. Answer me before the Lord and before his anointed: Whose ox or ass have I taken? Whom have I defrauded or whom have I oppressed? Or if I have taken a bribe from anyone's hand, even a shoe, speak out against me and I will restore it to you." And when the people answered: "You have not defrauded us or oppressed us or taken anything from anyone's hand," he called the Lord to witness, saying: "The Lord is witness, and his anointed is witness this

day that you have not found anything in my hands. And they said: He is witness" [1 Sam. 12:2–5]. In the same way, the apostle Paul wrote to the Corinthians displaying his good conscience: "For we are not like so many others who are adultering the word of God, but with sincerity, as coming from God, we speak before God in Christ. We have wronged no one, we have cheated no one" [2 Cor. 2:17; 7:2].

The church nourishes presbyters of this kind. The prophet says of them: "I will establish your princes in peace and your bishops in righteousness" [Isa. 60:17]. To them the Lord's word applies: "Who then is the faithful steward, good and wise, whom the Lord has set over his household, to give them their food at the proper time? Blessed is that servant whom the Lord when he comes will find so doing" [Matt. 24:45–46]. Paul teaches us where we may find such servants: "God has appointed in the church first apostles, second prophets, third teachers" [1 Cor. 12:28]. Thus, where God's charisms have their place, there the truth must be learned from those in whom all these signs are clearly present: the church's succession deriving from the apostles; a sound and irreproachable conduct; and an unadulterated, uncorrupted proclamation. For they guard our faith in the one God who created all things. They increase the love toward the Son of God who accomplished such marvelous dispensations for our sake. And they interpret the Scriptures for us without danger, uttering no blasphemies against God, or dishonoring the patriarchs, or despising the prophets.

V.

Origen

ON FIRST PRINCIPLES: BOOK FOUR

(Philocalia, Title)
The divinely inspired character
of Holy Scripture
and how it ought to be read and understood;
further, the reason for
the obscurity in it and
for statements in some passages
which are impossible and meaningless
according to the
literal sense.

I.

(I, 1) In our investigation of such weighty matters we are not content with common notions and the evidence of things one can see. Rather, from Scriptures that we believe to be divine, the so-called Old as well as the New Testament, we adduce testimonies as witnesses to that which we consider a convincing proof of our statements. Since we also attempt to confirm our faith by reason and since we have not yet discussed the divinity of the Scriptures, let us comment briefly on this topic, spelling out for this purpose the reasons which move us to speak of those writings as divine. First of all, even before we use the text and the content of these writings themselves, we must treat of Moses, the lawgiver of the Hebrews, and of Jesus Christ, the originator of the saving teachings of Christianity.

Despite the fact that there have been many legislators among Greeks and barbarians, and that numerous teachers have advocated doctrines laying claim to the truth, we have not come across any lawgiver who has been able to inspire zeal for the acceptance of his words among other nations. And while those who profess to be concerned with truth in their philosophy have introduced a whole arsenal of arguments as part of their alleged rational demonstration, none of them has been able to excite different nations, or even significant portions of a single nation, for that which he considers to be the truth. Yet, had this been possible, the legislators would gladly have extended to the entire human race the validity of the laws they regarded as good. The teachers, for their part, would have loved to disseminate all over the world what they imagined to be the truth. But since they could not persuade people speaking other languages and belonging to so many other nations to observe their laws and accept their teachings, they did not even dare to make a start in this direction; they concluded, not unreasonably, that it would be impossible for them to succeed in any such endeavor. Yet the entire inhabited world of Greek and barbarian nations is teeming with thousands of people who are eager to follow us, who abandon their traditional laws and their presumed deities for the observance of the law of Moses and for the instruction offered in the words of Jesus Christ. This is happening despite the fact that the followers of the law of Moses encounter the hatred of idol worshipers, and those who accept the word of Jesus Christ even risk the sentence of death in addition to that hatred.

(I, 2) We must keep before our eyes what is happening: in spite of constant anti-Christian machinations which cause some confessors of Christianity to lose their lives and others to lose their possessions, it has been possible for the word to be preached throughout the inhabited world even in the absence of an abundant supply of teachers, and Greeks and barbarians, wise and unwise, have adopted the religion proclaimed by Jesus. When we consider this situation we will not hesitate to call the achievement superhuman. Now, Jesus himself taught with all authority and persuasive power that the word would take hold. There is good reason, therefore, to regard also other utterances of his as divine predictions, for example: "You will be dragged before kings and governors for my sake to bear testimony before them and the nations" [Matt. 10:18], and: "On that day many will say to me: Lord, Lord, did we not eat in your name and drink in your name and cast out demons in your name? Then I will declare to them: Depart from me, you evildoers, I never knew you" [Matt. 7:22; Luke 13:26–27]. At the time, it might have seemed as if the one who uttered these words spoke in vain, that is, as if his words would not come true. Now, however, with the fulfillment of that which he had announced with such great authority, we have a clear indication that God has truly become man and has passed on to humans his teachings of salvation.

(I, 3) And what about the prophecy that "men called princes from Judah and rulers from his loins will be lacking when he comes for whom it has been reserved—obviously the kingdom!—and when the expectation of the nations is present" [Gen. 49:10]? From history and from our observation today it is clearly evident that no kings have ruled over the Jews ever since the times of Jesus. In fact, all the institutions in which the Jews took pride have been destroyed; things like the temple, the altar for the sacrifices, the cultic celebrations, and the garments of the high priest. Yes, (Hosea's) prophecy has been fulfilled: "For many days the sons of Israel will sit there without king and without ruler, without sacrifice, without altar, without priesthood, without oracular gear" [Hos. 3:4].

We use this latter text also against those who are embarrassed over the words of Jacob to Joseph in the Genesis text and argue that an ethnarch from the tribe of Judah is still ruling the people and will not lack progeny until the advent of the Messiah of which they are dreaming. For if "the sons of Israel will sit there for many days without king and without ruler, without sacrifice, without altar, without priesthood, without oracular gear," and if from the time the temple was razed to the ground there has been no sacrifice, no altar, and no priesthood, then it is plain that "a prince from Judah and a ruler from his loins" has in fact been lacking. But when the prophecy says: "A prince from Judah and a ruler from his loins will not be lacking until the coming of that which has been reserved for him," it is evident that he has come who possesses "that which has been reserved," he who is the expectation of the nations. Evidence of this last point is also presented by the host of Gentiles who have come to faith in God through Christ.

(I, 4) Furthermore, a prophetic statement in the Song of Deuteronomy reveals the future election of foolish nations as a result of the sins of the former people of God, an election which has been effected through none other but Jesus. It reads: "They have stirred me to jealousy with that which is not God; they have provoked me with their idols. Therefore, I will stir them to jealousy with that which is no people; I will provoke them with a foolish nation" [Deut. 32:21]. It is easy enough to see how the Hebrews who, as it says here, have stirred God to jealousy "with that which is not God" and provoked him with their idols have in turn been provoked to jealousy "with that which is no people," with a "foolish nation" elected by God through the advent of Christ and his disciples. We Gentiles only need to "consider our calling: not many were wise according to worldly standards, not many were powerful, not many were of noble birth; but God chose what is foolish in the world to shame the wise, and God chose what is lowly and despised, even things that are not, to bring to nothing things that formerly were, so that Israel according to the flesh"—the apostle simply calls it flesh—"might not boast in the presence of God" [1 Cor. 1:26–29].

(I, 5) But what about the prophecies concerning Christ which we find in the Psalms? One of the poems is addressed "to the Beloved"; his tongue is called "the pen of a ready scribe, fairer in beauty than the sons of men," for "grace is poured out upon his lips" [Ps. 45:1–2, LXX]. An indication of the "grace poured out upon his lips" is the fact that, despite the brief duration of his teaching—he taught for about one year and a few months—the inhabited world now is filled with his teaching and with the religion he brought. For "in his days righteousness has risen and an abundance of peace" which will last to the consummation, the "taking away of the moon," as the psalmist calls it; and "he continues to have dominion from sea to sea, and from the rivers to the ends of the earth" [Ps. 72:7–8, LXX]. Indeed, a sign has been given to the house of David; for "the virgin has conceived in her womb and has born a son, and his name is Immanuel which means: God with us" [Isa. 7:13–14]. The sign has been fulfilled just as the words of the same prophet announced it: "God is with us! Know it, you nations, and admit your defeat; you who are strong, admit your defeat!" [Isa. 8:8–9]; indeed, we Gentiles who have been won over by the grace of his word have been defeated, have been conquered! Even the place of his birth was predicted by Micah: "And you Bethlehem of the land of Judah are by no means the least among the leaders of Judah; for from you shall come a ruler who will shepherd my people Israel" [Matt. 2:6; cf. Micah 5:2]. Moreover, the seventy weeks which were to elapse before the coming of the messianic ruler, according to Daniel [Dan. 4:25], have reached their end. There has arrived, in the words of Job, the one "who has subdued the great sea-monster" [Job 3:8]; he has given his true disciples authority "to tread upon serpents and scorpions, and over all the power of the enemy" without their being hurt in any way [Luke 10:19]. We must consider only how the apostles, sent out by Jesus to announce the gospel, traveled all over the world, and we will realize both that this bold project surpassed human measure and that Christ's command was divine. Indeed, when we examine how people listening to the new teachings and the unfamiliar words were thwarted in their desire to plot against the apostles by a divine power protecting them and came to believe them, we will not doubt that the apostles did perform miracles because "God bore witness to their words by signs and wonders and various miracles" [Heb. 2:4].

(I, 6) In demonstrating the divinity of Jesus in this somewhat summary fashion by using prophetic pronouncements about him, we also offer proof that the Scriptures which prophesy about him are inspired and that those writings that announce his coming and his teaching speak with full power and authority; this is the reason they have won over the elect from among the nations. It must be admitted, however, that the divine quality of the prophetic statements and the spiritual character of the law of Moses came to light only with the coming of Jesus. Before Christ's advent it was hardly possible to present clear evidence that the old writings were inspired. But the coming of Jesus opened the eyes of readers who might have been skeptical about the divinity of the law and the prophets to the fact that these writings were indeed composed with the help of divine grace. Everyone who approaches the prophetic words attentively and diligently will experience a trace of divine enthusiasm in the very act of reading; the experience will convince him that what we believe to be God's words are not human writings. The light present in the law of Moses but previously hidden under a veil has begun to shine forth with the advent of Christ. The veil has been removed, and the good things whose shadow the letter displayed have gradually been raised to the status of knowledge [cf. 2 Cor. 3:13–16; Heb. 10:1].

(I, 7) At this point it would be too much of a task to review the age-old prophecies about every future event so that the skeptic, impressed by their divine quality, might leave behind all hesitation and uncertainty and open his soul fully to the words of God. It should not come as a surprise, however, that the superhuman quality of scriptural thoughts does not readily appear to the unskilled reader in each and every passage. Even among the works of providence, a providence which extends over the entire universe, some manifest their providential character very clearly, while others conceal it so much that they seem to leave room for a rejection of faith in the God who governs all with such marvelous skill and power. Things on earth do not manifest the artful operation of the provident God as clearly as sun, moon, and stars; the occurrences in the human sphere demonstrate it less cogently than a consideration of the souls and bodies of animals. Any interested observer can easily discover the "what for" and "why" when he investigates the instincts, mental images, and natural conditions of animals and the makeup of their bodies. But just as providence is not defrauded by that which we do not know, at least not in the eyes of those who accept it as a given reality, so the divinity of Scripture which extends to all its parts loses nothing by the fact that in our weakness we cannot discern at every turn of the letter the hidden splendor of doctrines concealed in the lowly and contemptible literal phrase. "For we have here a treasure in earthen

vessels so that the abundance of God's power may shine forth"
and may not be regarded as coming from us who are human
beings [2 Cor. 4:7]. If the sterile methods of demonstration
which are prominent in the books of human authors had pre-
vailed over human minds, there would be good reason to suspect our faith of being based on human wisdom, not on the
wisdom of God. But now it is obvious to anyone who does not
close his eyes that the word and its proclamation have proved
their might among so many people "not in plausible words of
wisdom but in the manifestation of the spirit and of power" [2
Cor. 2:4]. Therefore, since a heavenly or rather a superheavenly
power drives us to worship him alone who created us, let us
strive to "leave behind the basic teaching about Christ," that is,
the elementary instruction; let us go on to perfection [Heb.
5:12; 6:1] so that the wisdom spoken among the perfect may be
spoken among us also. For the apostle who had found wisdom
promised to proclaim wisdom among the perfect, a wisdom different from the wisdom of this age and of its rulers, an age
which is doomed to pass away [1 Cor. 2:6]. We will bear the
distinct imprint of this wisdom "according to the revelation of
the mystery which was kept in silence for eternal ages but is
now disclosed through the prophetic writings and the appearance of our Lord and Savior Jesus Christ. To him be glory into all
ages. Amen" [Rom. 16:25–27].

II.

(II, 1) Having explained briefly that the divine writings are
inspired, we must now turn to the discussion of the manner in
which they must be read and understood. For innumerable
errors have arisen because so many people have failed to find
the right path which must govern the exploration of the holy
books.

On the one hand, those advocates of circumcision whose
hearts were hardened and who had no understanding refused to
believe in our Savior. It was their intention to follow the letter of
the prophecies which spoke of him, but they did not see him
physically "proclaiming release to the captives" [Isa. 61:1], or
"building the city" [Ps. 46:4–5, LXX] which they take to be the

actual city of God, or "cutting off the chariots from Ephraim and the war horse from Jerusalem" [Zech. 9:10], or "eating butter and honey and, before knowing and giving preference to evil, choosing the good" [Isa. 7:15–16]. They also thought that the prophecy was referring to the four-footed animal called a wolf when it said that "the wolf shall graze with the lamb, and the leopard shall lie down with the kid and the little calf, and steer and lion shall feed together led by a little child, and ox and bear shall go to pasture together, and the lion shall eat straw like the ox" [Isa. 11:6–7]. Failing to see any of this happening in a physical sense at the advent of the one whom we believe to be the Christ, they did not accept our Lord Jesus but crucified him as one who had claimed to be the Messiah against the law.

On the other hand, when the advocates of heresies were reading passages like: "A fire is kindled in my anger" [Jer. 15:14]; "I am a jealous God visiting the sins of the fathers upon the children to the third and fourth generation" [Exod. 20:5]; "I repent that I have anointed Saul king" [1 Sam. 15:10]; "I am a God who makes peace and who creates evil" [Isa. 45:7]; or: "There is no evil in the city which the Lord has not done" [Amos 3:6]; "evil has come down from the Lord upon the gates of Jerusalem" [Micah 1:12]; "an evil spirit from God suffocated Saul" [1 Sam. 18:10], and a host of similar texts, they did not dare to doubt that such Scriptures were the writings of God; but they attributed them to the creator-god *(dēmiourgos)* whom the Jews worship. Since this creator-god is imperfect and not good, they reasoned that the Savior had come proclaiming a more perfect God who, as they maintain, is not the creator-god, and of whom they hold various opinions. Once they forsook the creator who is the unbegotten and only God, they became lost in the fictions of their own minds and fashioned their own mythical theories about how they thought the visible creation and certain invisible realities of which their soul had formed an image had come into existence.

In contrast to this speculation, even the simplest minds among those proud to belong to the church have never assumed the existence of any god greater than the creator-god. This, of course, is a sound attitude on their part. But they do attribute to him features which they would not attribute even to the most cruel and unjust human being.

(II, 2) The reason for the false opinions, the impious attitudes, and the amateurish talk about God on the part of those groups just mentioned seems to be no other than that Scripture is not understood in its spiritual sense but is interpreted according to the mere letter. All those, therefore, who are convinced that the holy books are not the writings of human authors but were composed and have come down to us as a result of the inspiration of the Holy Spirit by the will of the Father of All through Jesus Christ, and who adhere to the rule of the celestial church of Christ resting on the succession of the apostles, must be taught what I take to be the correct method of interpretation.

Now, everyone who embraces the word, even the dullest of all, is convinced that there are certain mystical arrangements *(oikonomiai)* which the divine writings reveal to us. The prudent and unpretentious, however, admit that they do not know what these mysteries comprise. If, for example, someone raises questions about Lot's sexual relations with his daughters, about Abraham's two wives, about the two sisters married to Jacob, or about the two maidservants who had children by him, they will simply reply that there are mysteries here which our mind cannot fathom. Yet when they read about the construction of the tabernacle, convinced that the scriptural account has typical significance, they try to find the reality which corresponds to every detail mentioned in that story. They are quite correct in their conviction that the tabernacle is the "type" of something. But they sometimes get lost in their attempt to apply the word to this or that specific reality of which the tabernacle is a type without violating the dignity of Scripture. They assert that every narrative which on the surface seems to concern marriages, childbirths, wars, or other events which the multitude would accept as historical, does present types. But when we ask: types of what? then, partly because of insufficient skill, partly because of undue haste, but sometimes even in spite of all the skill and patience of the interpreter, those questions about the meaning of each detail remain largely unanswered since it is so extremely difficult for human minds to identify the specific realities intended.

(II, 3) What should we say about the prophecies which we all know are full of enigmatic and dark expressions [cf. Prov. 1:6]? Even the precise sense of the Gospels as a reflection of the "mind of Christ" requires the grace granted to the apostle who said: "But we have the mind of Christ that we might understand the gracious gifts bestowed on us by God, and we impart it in words not taught by human wisdom but by the Spirit" [1 Cor. 2:16, 12–13]. And who can read the revelations granted to John without being amazed at the hidden depth of the ineffable mysteries, a depth apparent even to the person who does not understand what the text says? Which expert in the art of careful textual analysis would find the letters of the apostles clear and easy to understand, when even here innumerable instances afford nothing more than a fleeting glimpse, a view as through a tiny hole, of a host of most sublime thoughts.

Since this is the situation and since so many people go astray, it is quite dangerous to assert that the reader easily catches the meaning of texts which require the key of knowledge. This key is in the hand of the lawyers, the Savior says. If anyone is unwilling to admit that before the advent of Christ the truth was in the hands of the lawyers, let him explain to us how our Lord Jesus Christ can say that the key of knowledge is in their hands, in the hands of people who, according to our skeptics, do not have books containing the ineffable and perfect mysteries of knowledge. This is what the text says: "Woe to you lawyers, for you have taken away the key of knowledge; you did not enter yourselves, and you hindered those who were entering" [Luke 11:52].

(II, 4) Indeed, it seems to us that the correct method of approaching the Scriptures and grasping their sense is the following, taking it from the texts themselves. In the Proverbs of Solomon we find this kind of directive concerning divine doctrines in Scripture: "And you, write down those things threefold in your counsel and wisdom that you may reply with words of truth to those who ask you" [Prov. 22:20–21]. This means, one should inscribe on one's soul the intentions of the holy literature in a threefold manner; the simpler person might be edified by the flesh of Scripture, as it were (flesh is our designation for the obvious understanding), the somewhat more advanced by its soul, as it were; but the person who is perfect and approaches the apostle's description: "Among the perfect we impart wisdom although it is not a wisdom of this age or of the rulers of this age who are doomed to pass away; but we impart a secret and hidden wisdom of God which God decreed before the ages for our glorification" [1 Cor. 2:6–7], by the spiritual law which contains "a shadow of the good things to come" [Heb. 10:1]. For just as the human being consists of body, soul, and spirit, so does Scripture which God has arranged to be given for the salvation of humankind.

We also apply this exegesis to a story in the *Shepherd* (of Hermas), a book despised by some. Hermas is ordered to write two books and then to announce to the elders of the church what he has learned from the Spirit. The text reads as follows: "You shall write two books, and you shall give one to Clement and one to Graptē. And Graptē shall admonish the widows and orphans; but Clement shall send it to the cities outside. You, however, shall announce it to the elders of the church" [Hermas, *Vision* II.4.3]. Now Graptē, the woman who admonishes the widows and orphans, stands for the mere letter exhorting those whose souls are children and who are still unable to address God as Father—this is the reason they are called orphans. She also admonishes those who no longer live with an illegitimate husband but are still widows because they have not yet become worthy of the bridegroom. Clement, who already stands outside the letter, is told to transmit the message to the "cities outside"; we may interpret these as souls who have left the realm of bodily concerns and base thoughts. Hermas himself, the disciple of the Spirit, is ordered to announce the message to "the elders" of the church of God as a whole, to men who have turned gray with insight; he is to address them no longer through the written letter but through living words.

(II, 5) But since some scriptural passages have no bodily sense at all, as we shall show in the following section, there are cases where one must seek only for the soul and the spirit of the passage, so to speak. Perhaps this is why the stone jars which are reported to be set up for the purification of the Jews hold "two or three measures each," as we read in the Gospel of John [John

2:6]. The expression hints at those whom the apostle calls "Jews inwardly" [Rom. 2:29]; they are purified through the word of the Scriptures which sometimes hold two measures—the psychic sense, if I may say so, and the pneumatic sense—sometimes three; for, in addition to the two just mentioned, certain texts also possess a bodily sense which may be edifying. The mention of six jars makes good sense; the reference is to those who are being purified in the world which was created in six days, a perfect number.

(II, 6) The large number of Christians whose faith is genuine but somewhat simple testifies that one can draw profit even from the first understanding; it is indeed helpful to an extent. On the other hand, Paul in his First Epistle to the Corinthians provides an illustration of the kind of interpretation which leads up to the soul, as it were: "It is written," he says, "you shall not muzzle an ox when it is treading out the grain"; and he adds as an interpretation of this law: "Is it for oxen that God is concerned? Does he not speak entirely for our sake? It was written for our sake because the plowman should plow in hope and the thresher thresh in hope of a share in the crop" [1 Cor. 9:9-10]. Most current interpretations which suit the multitude and edify those unable to listen to higher truths have something of the same character.

Spiritual exegesis, however, is reserved for the one who can identify the heavenly realities, whose copy and shadow the "Jews according to the flesh" were worshiping, and who can recognize the good things to come of which the law displays but a shadow [Heb. 8:5; 10:1]. In one word, the apostolic challenge is this: We must seek in everything "the secret and hidden wisdom of God, which God decreed before the ages for the glorification of the righteous and which none of the rulers of this age understood" [1 Cor. 2:7-8]. The same apostle says elsewhere, after quoting certain passages from Exodus and Numbers: "These things happened to them as a type, but they were written down for our sake, upon whom the end of the ages has come" [1 Cor. 10:11]. He even provides clues to the realities of which those events were types when he says: "For they drank from the spiritual rock which followed them, and the rock was

Christ" [1 Cor. 10:4]. And when he outlines the details of the tabernacle in another letter, he quotes: "Make everything according to the pattern which was shown to you on the mountain" [Heb. 8:5; Exod. 25:40]. On the other hand, in the Epistle to the Galatians he is in a way chiding those who think they are reading the law, but who do not understand it. His verdict is that those who do not understand the law are those who think there are no allegories in the biblical texts. "Tell me," he says, "you who desire to be under a law, do you not hear the law? For it is written that Abraham had two sons, one by a slave and one by a free woman. But the son of the slave woman was born according to the flesh, the son of the free woman through the promise. Now this is an allegory; these women are two covenants," and so on [Gal. 4:21–24]. One must pay close attention to every turn of the phrase here. Paul says: "you who desire to be under a law," not "you who are under the law"; and: "do you not hear the law?", hearing being judged by understanding and knowing. In the Epistle to the Colossians he summarizes the hidden agenda of the entire legislation in a few words by saying: "Therefore, let no one pass judgment on you in questions of food and drink or with regard to a festival or a new moon or a sabbath with their partial character. These are only shadows of what is to come" [Col. 2:16–17]. Furthermore, speaking of those who practice circumcision, he writes in the Epistle to the Hebrews: "They worship a copy and shadow of the heavenly things" [Heb. 8:5].

It is likely, therefore, that those who accept the apostle once and for all as a man of God *(theios anēr)* will not be in doubt about the five books attributed to Moses. But they want to know whether the rest of the historical narrative also happened as a type. At this point, one must pay close attention to a quotation in the Epistle to the Romans which comes from the third book of Kings: "I have kept for myself seven thousand men who have not bowed the knee to Baal" [Rom. 11:5; 1 Kings 19:18]. Paul understood this as a reference to those who are Israelites by God's election, since not only the Gentiles but also some of God's own nation profited by the coming of Christ.

(II, 7) With this situation in mind we must outline the characteristics of a proper understanding of the Scriptures as we see them. First, we must point out that the goal *(skopos)* of the Spirit who, under God's providence, enlightened the prophets and apostles, those servants of the truth, through the Word which was with God in the beginning [John 1:1–2], was concerned primarily with the ineffable mysteries surrounding the fate of humans; by humans here I mean souls making use of bodies. His purpose was that, by carefully searching the plain texts and taking seriously the depth of their meaning, every teachable person would have a part in all the teachings of his counsel. But if the topic of the discussion is souls who cannot achieve perfection apart from the rich and profound truth about God, then the teachings concerning God himself must necessarily take first place, as must those concerning his only-begotten Son. We must ask what his nature is; in what sense he is the Son of God; for what reasons he descended as far down as the level of human flesh and completely assumed humanity; what his work is, and for whom and when it is exercised. By the same necessity something about other rational beings akin to us, both those who are more divine and those who have fallen from the state of blessedness, and something about the causes of their fall had to be included in the words of divine instruction. Something also had to be said about the difference between souls, the origin of these differences, the nature of the world, and the reason for its existence. Furthermore, we need to be instructed about the origin of so much terrible evil on earth, and whether it is found not only on earth but elsewhere as well.

(II, 8) While these and similar topics were the primary concern of the Spirit enlightening the souls of the holy servants of truth, he had a second goal for the benefit of those who cannot carry the workload which the discovery of such matters requires. This goal was to hide his teachings about the above-mentioned issues in texts which on the surface seemed to offer a plain narrative account of events such as the creation of the sensible world, the fashioning of man, and of the successive generations from the first parents to a multiplicity of human beings; the same holds true for other historical narratives which record the deeds of righteous people and of the mistakes they some-times made because they were human beings, but also the wicked deeds, the licentious acts, and the greedy behavior of lawless and godless people. Most astonishing of all, even the stories of wars, of victors and vanquished, can disclose some ineffable (mysteries) to those who know how to examine such accounts with care. And still more marvelous: through a written code of law the true laws are being announced prophetically; and all of this is written down in proper order with a power truly befitting the wisdom of God. The intent was that the external cover of spiritual things, namely, the bodily element of the Scriptures, should not be rendered unprofitable for so many people; but rather, that it should be capable of improving the multitude according to their capacity.

(II, 9) But if the usefulness of the legal prescriptions as well as the logical coherence and the smooth flow of the historical nar-rative were automatically evident everywhere, we would not believe that it is possible to find some other sense in the Scrip-tures besides the obvious one. For this reason the Word of God has arranged the insertion of certain offensive features, of stum-bling blocks and impossibilities amid the law and historical nar-rative. He wanted to avoid that, being totally carried away by the plain text and its unspoiled charm, we either would disregard its teachings altogether because we did not find any lessons worthy of God, or would refuse to move beyond the letter and not learn anything more divine.

One must also be aware of another feature. Since the (Spirit's) primary goal was to present the logical system of spiritual reali-ties by means of events that happened and things that were to be done, the Word used actual historical events wherever they could be accommodated to these mystical (meanings), hiding the deeper sense from the multitude. But where the recorded actions of a specific person did not fit the account of the inner coherence of intelligible realities in terms of the deeper mysti-cal meaning, Scripture has woven into the historical narrative some feature which did not happen; sometimes the event is an impossibility; sometimes, though possible, it actually did not happen. Sometimes only a few phrases which are not true in the bodily sense are inserted, sometimes more. We must assume an analogous situation in regard to the law. Frequently one can find commandments which are useful in themselves and appropriate for the time of legislation. Sometimes, however, their usefulness is not self-evident. At other times, even impossible things are commanded; such instances challenge the more skillful and inquisitive to devote themselves to a painstaking examination of the text and become seriously convinced that a sense worthy of God needs to be sought in these commandments.

But the Spirit made such arrangements not only with regard to the period before the advent of Christ; being the same Spirit and coming from the one God, he acted similarly when dealing with the Gospels and apostles. Even they did not present the historical narrative completely free of additions which did not actually happen; nor did they always transmit the legal prescriptions and the commandments in such a way that they seem reasonable in themselves.

III.

(III, 1) To be specific: What intelligent person can believe that there was a first day, then a second and third day, evening, and morning, without the sun, the moon, and the stars; and the first day—if this is the right term—even without a heaven [Gen. 1:5–6]? Who is foolish enough to believe that, like a human farmer, God planted a garden to the east in Eden and created in it a visible, physical tree of life from which anyone tasting its fruit with bodily teeth would receive life; and that one would have a part in good and evil by eating the fruit picked from the appropriate tree [Gen. 2:8 – 9]? When God is depicted walking in the garden in the evening and Adam hiding behind the tree, I think no one will doubt that these details point figuratively to some mysteries by means of a historical narrative which seems to have happened but did not happen in a bodily sense. By the same token, when Cain "went out from the face of the Lord" [Gen. 4:16], it is quite clear to the insightful that this expression stimulates the careful reader to inquire what the face of God is and what it means for someone to go out from it. What more needs to be said? Those who are not totally dull can collect innumerable examples of this kind, where something is presented as having happened but did not happen in terms of the literal meaning of the text.

Even the Gospels are full of passages of this kind, such as the devil leading Jesus up to a high mountain in order to show him from there all the kingdoms of the world and their glory [Matt. 4:8]. Now who but the most superficial reader of a story like this would not laugh at those who think that the kingdoms of the Persians, the Scythians, the Indians, and the Parthians as well as the way their rulers receive glory from their subjects can be seen with the eye of the flesh which requires elevation in order to perceive things located down below? The thorough investigator can find enough similar instances to convince himself that stories which happened according to the letter are interspersed with other events which did not actually occur.

(III, 2) When we come to the legislation of Moses, if one attempts to observe it as it stands, many laws speak nonsense and others command the impossible. It makes no sense to forbid the eating of vultures [Lev. 11:4]; even during the worst famines the lack of food has never forced anyone yet to resort to eating this animal. Or, there is the command to cut off uncircumcised children of eight days from their people; it really should be their fathers or foster parents who ought to be killed if any literal law at all had to be given for this case. Yet Scripture actually says: "Any uncircumcised male who is not circumcised on the eighth day shall be cut off from his people" [Gen. 17:4].

If you wish to see impossible things being commanded in the law, let me point out that the goatstag *(tragelaphos)* is an example of an animal which cannot exist; yet Moses decrees to sacrifice it as a clean animal [Deut. 14:5]. Moreover, the griffin is not reported ever to have fallen into human hands; yet the lawgiver forbids eating it [Deut. 14:12; Lev. 11:3]. Also, concerning the much-discussed Sabbath (rest), if one is scrupulous about the commandment, "sit down every one of you in your homes; let no one of you leave his place on the seventh day" [Exod. 16:29], one will find it impossible to observe literally; no creature can remain seated for a whole day and not move from a sitting position. Therefore, the people of the circumcision and all who maintain that nothing beyond the literal reading of the text has been revealed never bother to ask questions about certain matters such as the goatstag, the griffin, and the vulture. But about other things they chatter with sophistical ingenuity, adducing silly traditions; concerning the Sabbath, for example, they say that each person's "place" measures two thousand cubits. Others, the Samaritan Dositheos among them, reject this interpretation and believe that one must remain until evening in the very position in which one has been caught by the Sabbath day. Just as impossible is the command not to carry a burden on the Sabbath [Jer. 17:22]. Concerning this matter the teachers of the Jews have engaged in an interminable argument, claiming that one kind of footwear is a burden but another kind is not; the sandal with hobnails is, but the sandal without hobnails is not; a load carried on one shoulder is a burden, but a load carried on both shoulders is not.

(III, 3) When we come to the Gospel and look for parallels, what could be more unreasonable than the command which simple minds think the Savior gave to his apostles: "Salute no one on the road" [Luke 10:4]? The saying about the right cheek being struck [Matt. 5:39; Luke 6:29] is also most unlikely, for anyone who strikes would strike the left cheek with the right hand unless he happened to suffer from an unnatural condition. Moreover, it is impossible to accept the Gospel notion of plucking out the right eye if it causes offense [Matt. 5:29]. For even if we grant that someone might be offended by seeing, why is only the right eye at fault when both eyes see? Who, accusing himself of looking lustfully at a woman [Matt. 5:28], would attribute the fault to the right eye alone and have a good reason to pluck it out? In fact, even the apostle decrees (an impossibility) when he says: "Was anyone already circumcised at the time of his call? Let him not undo the marks of his circumcision" [1 Cor. 7:18]. First, anyone who pays attention will notice that this saying has no connection with the subject under discussion. In the context where the apostle is laying down rules about marriage and celibacy the remark strikes one as being thrown in at random. Second, who would speak of wrongdoing if a person would undergo an operation to have the marks of circumcision removed, if possible, when circumcision is a disgrace in the opinion of the multitude?

(III, 4) We mention all these examples in order to show that the purpose of the divine power offering us the holy Scriptures is not only that we understand what the plain text presents to us, for, taken literally, it is sometimes not only untrue but even unreasonable and impossible. We wanted to show also that some extraneous matter has been woven into the historical narrative of actual events and into the code of laws which are useful in their literal sense. No one, however, should suspect us of generalizing and saying that because a particular story did not happen, no story actually happened; or that, because a particular law is unreasonable or impossible in its plain reading, no law should be observed literally; or that the scriptural stories about the Savior are untrue in terms of the physical reality; or that none of the laws and commandments which he gave ought to be obeyed. On the contrary, it must be emphasized that the factual truth of the historical narrative is presented to us quite clearly in certain texts; for example that Abraham was buried in the double cave at Hebron as were Isaac and Jacob and one wife of each [Gen. 23:19; 25:9–10; 49:29–32; 50:13]; that Shechem was given as a portion to Joseph [Josh. 24:32; Gen. 48:22]; that Jerusalem is the capital of Judea, and Solomon built there a temple of the Lord [1 Kings 6], and a host of other instances. In fact, instances which are true in terms of the historical narrative far outnumber the purely spiritual texts which have been woven in. Who would not admit that the commandment, "honor your father and your mother that it may be well with you" [Exod. 20:12], is useful without any anagogy and ought to be kept, when even the apostle Paul refers to it verbatim [Eph. 6:2–3]? What more needs to be said about the others: "You shall not kill; you shall not commit adultery; you shall not steal; you shall not bear false witness" [Exod. 20:13–16]? Furthermore, we find commandments in the Gospels about which we do not even question whether or not they should be observed literally, for example: "But I say to you, everyone who is angry with his brother," and so on [Matt. 5:22], and: "But I say to you, do not swear at all" [Matt. 5:34]. Likewise, the word of the apostle must be kept literally: "Admonish the idle, encourage the faint-hearted, help the weak, be patient with them all" [1 Thess. 5:14], even though each of these exhortations, without being set aside in its literal meaning, may also preserve certain "depths of the wisdom of God" [Rom. 11:33] for the more ambitious.

(III, 5) The conscientious interpreter, however, will be in a quandary in certain cases; he will be unable to decide without painstaking examination whether a particular incident claimed to be historical actually happened as the text reads, or whether the letter of a particular law should be obeyed or not. The conscientious reader who observes the Savior's command, "Search the Scriptures!" [John 5:39] must therefore carefully examine where the literal sense is true and where it is impossible. He must search out as far as he can the sense of those passages which are impossible according to the plain text, a sense scattered throughout Scripture, beginning his examination with expressions resembling each other. It will be clear to him that a serious effort must be made to comprehend the sense of a text as a whole when the textual sequence taken literally is impossible, yet its primary sense is not impossible but true. In such cases he must provide the connection on the level of intelligible reality between a statement impossible in its literal sense and those statements which are not only possible but true according to the historical narrative, allegorizing the latter along with the texts which did not happen according to the letter. For with regard to divine Scripture as a whole we are of the opinion that all of it has a spiritual sense, but not all of it has a bodily sense. In fact, in many cases the bodily sense proves to be impossible. This is the reason so much diligence must be applied by the person approaching the divine books reverently as divine writings. To me, this mode of understanding seems to be the correct one.

(III, 6) The biblical accounts state that on earth God elected a nation which is given a variety of names. As a whole, this nation is called Israel; it is also called Jacob. When it was divided at the time of Jeroboam son of Nabat, the ten tribes reportedly under his rule took the name of Israel, while the two others together with Levi, ruled by kings of Davidic descent, took the name of

Judah. The entire area settled by the members of this nation and given to them by God is called Judea. Its chief city is Jerusalem, obviously the mother city *(mētropolis)* of several others whose names one finds scattered in many places here and there but combined into a single list in the (book of) Joshua the son of Nun [Joshua 13—21]. Against this background, the apostle states somewhere, raising our discursive insight to a higher level: "Consider Israel according to the flesh" [1 Cor. 10:18]; he implies that there may be also an Israel according to the spirit. Elsewhere he says: "For it is not the children of the flesh who are the children of God, and not all who are descended from Israel are Israel" [Rom. 9:8, 6]; and: "The one is not a real Jew who is a Jew outwardly, nor is true circumcision something external and physical. He is a Jew who is one inwardly, and real circumcision is a matter of the heart; in the spirit, not in the letter" [Rom. 2:28–29]. Now, if the criterion for the Jew is found in something inward, we must understand that just as there is a race of the Jews in the flesh, there is also a nation of the Jews inwardly, the soul having acquired this noble lineage through certain ineffable words. Moreover, many prophecies speak of Israel and Judah, predicting what will happen to them. Now, do these great scriptural promises to them, unassuming as their text may be and lacking any display of the majesty and dignity of a promise from God, not require mystical anagogy? Certainly, if these promises refer to intelligible realities expressed through sensible realities, the recipients of the promises are not bodily either.

(III, 7) But let us not spend time on the discussion of the "Jew inwardly" and the inner Israelite. What has been said is sufficient for those whose mind is not dull. Returning to our topic, we remind ourselves that Jacob was the father of the twelve patriarchs; they were the fathers of the clan leaders, and these in turn became the fathers of the successive generations of Israelites. Thus, the bodily Israelites trace their origin back to the clan leaders, the clan leaders to the patriarchs, and the patriarchs to Jacob and his predecessors. Now, is it not true also that the intelligible Israelites, of whom the bodily Israelites are the type, derived from clans, and the clans derived from tribes, and the tribes from a single individual whose birth was not a bodily one but one of a higher order? He was born of Isaac who in turn descended from Abraham, and all go back to Adam who is Christ, as the Apostle says [1 Cor. 15:45]. For every lineage ranking below the God of All traces its origin to Christ. After the God and Father of All, he is the father of every soul just as Adam is the father of all human beings. If Paul could also interpret Eve anagogically as the church [Eph. 5:31–32?], it is not astonishing, although in the primary sense everyone is born of the church, that there are apostasies from the church since Cain was born of Eve and all succeeding generations go back to Eve.

(III, 8) If that which we hear about Israel and its tribes and clans is startling, we cannot understand the Savior's word, "I was sent only to the lost sheep of the house of Israel" [Matt. 15:24], in the manner of the Ebionites; they are poor in mental capacity, deriving their name from their poor intelligence— among the Hebrews, *ebiôn* is the word for a poor man. We do not suppose that Christ came primarily for the fleshly Israelites. For "not the children of the flesh are the children of God" [Rom. 9:8]. Moreover, about Jerusalem the apostle teaches something like the following: "The Jerusalem above is free; she is our mother" [Gal. 4:26], and in another epistle: "But you have come to Mount Zion and to the city of the living God, the heavenly Jerusalem, and to innumerable angels in festal gatherings, and to the assembly of the first-born who are enrolled in heaven" [Heb. 12:22–23]. Now if there is an Israel in the world of souls and a city of Jerusalem in heaven, it follows that the cities of Israel, and consequently all Judea, have as their mother city *(mētropolis)* the Jerusalem which is in heaven. Therefore, if we listen to Paul as one speaking for God and proclaiming wisdom, everything that is prophesied and said about Jerusalem must be understood as scriptural teaching about the heavenly city and its whole region, comprising the cities of the holy land. Perhaps the Savior points us to those cities anagogically when he mentions his giving authority over ten or five cities to those of whose stewardship over their pounds he approves [Luke 19:17–19].

(III, 9) Now if the prophecies concerning Judea and Jerusalem, Israel, Judah, and Jacob suggest mysteries of this kind when they are not taken in a fleshly sense, it would follow that the same is true of the prophecies concerning Egypt and the Egyptians, Babylon and the Babylonians, Tyre and the Tyreans, Sidon and the Sidonians, as well as all the other nations; they refer not only to the bodily Egyptians, Babylonians, Tyreans, and Sidonians. If there are Israelites in the realm of intelligibles, it follows that there are also intelligible Egyptians and Babylonians. What Ezekiel says about Pharaoh, king of Egypt [Ezekiel 29—32], does not really fit a person who ruled or was to rule over Egypt, as careful observers will notice. Likewise, his prophecy about the prince of Tyre cannot be taken to refer to a particular individual who was to rule over Tyre [Ezekiel 28]. And how can one understand the things that are said about Nebuchadnezzar in many places, especially in Isaiah, to refer to that particular individual? The historical Nebuchadnezzar did not fall from heaven; he was not the morning star, neither did he rise in the morning over the earth [Isa. 14:12]. Furthermore, when Ezekiel says of Egypt that it will be laid waste for forty years so that no human foot shall be found in it, and that it will be torn by war so terribly that the blood will flow knee-deep throughout the land [Ezekiel 29:10–12, 30–32], no intelligent person will understand this to refer to the land of Egypt bordering on the Ethiopians whose bodies are blackened by the sun.

(Rufinus) Instead, we must consider whether these passages cannot be understood in a more appropriate way. Just as there is a heavenly Jerusalem and Judea and no doubt a nation called Israel living in it, so it is possible that there are certain regions nearby called Egypt, Babylon, Tyre, or Sidon, and that their rulers and the souls perhaps living there are called Egyptians, Babylonians, Tyreans, and Sidonians. Among these souls some kind of captivity seems to have developed in accordance with the kind of life they lead there: they have come down, it says, from Judea to Babylon or to Egypt from better and higher places or have been dispersed among some other nations.

(Philocalia) (III, 10) We can perhaps say this: Those who die the common death here on earth and are judged to deserve placement in the so-called Hades are classified according to

their deeds down here and are then assigned different places in proportion to their sins. In the same way, those who die up there, if I may say so, descend into this (world as their) Hades and are judged to deserve varying abodes, better or worse, all over the region of this earth, with parents of one kind or another. Thus, an Israelite sometimes may fall among the Scythians, and an Egyptian may move over into Judea. But the Savior came to gather the lost sheep of the house of Israel [Matt. 15:24], and since many Israelites did not follow his teaching, the members of the (Gentile) nations are now called as well.

(Jerome) We have just compared the souls which descend from this world into the underworld to those souls who died, as it were, when they came down from a higher region to our habitations. Now we must examine very carefully whether the same can be said about the origin of individual souls. The souls born here have either come up to a higher world from the underworld and have taken a human body out of a renewed desire for improvement, or they have descended to us from better places. In the same way, other souls occupying the regions above in the firmament either have progressed from our habitations to better ones or have fallen from higher places as far down as the firmament, but their sins were not so great that they were thrown into the lower regions which we inhabit.

(Rufinus) The consequence seems to be that the prophecies pronounced over individual nations most likely refer to souls and their various celestial abodes. But we must also scrutinize and closely examine the historical accounts of events which befell the people of Israel, Jerusalem, or Judea, when one nation or another made war on them. In a great many instances it is not certain that they happened in a bodily sense. Therefore, we must ask how these events might be more appropriately applied to those nations of souls who either were dwelling in that heaven which is said to pass away, or must be assumed to dwell there even now.

(III, 11) But if someone asks us for self-evident, unambiguous proofs of these truths from the sacred Scriptures, our answer must be that the Holy Spirit decided to hide them more thoroughly and bury them more deeply in stories which seem to present historical accounts of actual events. These stories tell of people descending into Egypt and being held captive in Babylon, some being greatly humiliated in those regions and being forced into the service of slavemasters; they tell of others who rose to such fame and honor in the very places of their captivity that they achieved positions of power and rulership and were placed in charge of nations to govern them.

(Philocalia) All of this truth, we think, is hidden in the historical accounts. For "the kingdom of heaven is like treasure hidden in a field which the finder covered up; then in his joy he goes and sells all that he has and buys that field" [Matt. 13:44]. Let us consider whether this whole field overgrown with all kinds of plants is not the visible aspect of Scripture, that which lies on the surface and is readily accessible; its rich contents, however, which are not visible to all, are buried under the visible vegetation, as it were; they are the hidden treasures of wisdom and knowledge [Col. 2:3] which the Spirit through the prophet Isaiah calls "dark, invisible, and hidden." To find them, we need the God who alone can "break in pieces the doors of bronze" that hide them and can "cut asunder the bars of iron fastened to the doors" [Isa. 45:2–3]. Then all the truths hidden in Genesis can be discovered: What is said there about the various kinds of souls, authentic seeds, as it were, either close to Israel or far off; or about the descent of seventy souls into Egypt where they became as numerous as the stars of heaven [Gen. 46:26–27; Deut. 10:22]. But since not all of their descendants are the "light of the world" [Matt. 5:14], for "not all who are descended from Israel are Israel" [Rom. 9:6], there has grown a posterity from those seventy "as the innumerable grains of sand by the seashore" [Heb. 11:12].

(Rufinus) (III, 12) We may look upon God's providence as having permitted this descent of the holy fathers into Egypt, that is, into this world, for the enlightenment of others and the instruction of the human race; through them other souls should be enlightened and helped. They were the first to be entrusted with the oracles of God [Rom. 3:2] because Israel is the only nation that is said to "see God"; this is what the name Israel means in translation. It follows that other stories must be

adapted and interpreted accordingly: Egypt being struck by ten plagues so that it allows the people of God to depart; certain events befalling the people in the wilderness; the tabernacle being built and the robe of the high priest being woven with the contributions of the entire people; details being mentioned about the vessels of the temple cult since they really contain the shadow and type of heavenly things, as Scripture puts it: Paul clearly says of them that "they serve as a shadow and image of heavenly things" [Heb. 8:5]. Likewise, this same law spells out the rules and regulations by which the people must live in the holy land. There are threats against those who transgress the law. Furthermore, various kinds of ablutions are prescribed for those who need purification; the assumption is that they defile themselves time and again, and the prescription is meant to bring them finally to that one purification after which a person can no longer defile himself.

Furthermore, a census is taken of the people although not all are counted [Numbers 1]. The child souls have not yet reached the age to be counted according to the divine command. Neither are those souls counted who cannot become the head of another but are themselves subjected to others as their head; Scripture calls them "women." They are not included in the figures of that census which God commands; only those are counted who are called "men." This is intended to show that women souls cannot be counted separately but are included with those called "men." The census extends first of all to those ready to go forth to war for Israel. This means the ones who are able to fight against those hostile forces and enemies whom the Father subjects to the Son sitting at his right hand that he may destroy every rule and every power [1 Cor. 15:24, 27]. Through the number of these men, his warriors, who, "serving as God's soldiers do not get entangled in worldly pursuits" [2 Tim. 2:4], he will overturn the kingdoms of the adversary. They are to carry the shields of faith and to hurl the darts of wisdom; on them as their helmet gleams the hope of salvation, and the breastplate of love protects a bosom filled with God. To me this seems to be the kind of soldiers represented by those men who are ordered in the divine books to be counted according to

God's command, and this the kind of warfare for which they prepare.

But much more exalted and perfect than these are the ones of whom it is said that even the hairs of their head are numbered [Matt. 10:30]. On the other hand, those who were punished for their sins and whose bodies fell in the wilderness seem to symbolize the souls which made considerable progress but for various reasons were unable to reach the goal of perfection: they murmured, worshiped idols, and committed fornication, as Scripture says, or did abominable things which the mind should not be allowed even to conceive [cf. 1 Cor. 10:1ff.].

To me, even a detail like the following does not seem devoid of all mystery: Certain Israelites, owners of large herds of cattle and other animals, go ahead and snatch up beforehand a tract of land well suited for pasture and as grazing ground for their cattle; it was the first territory the right hand of the Israelite army had defended [Num. 32:1ff.]. They ask Moses for this land and live a separate existence on the other side of the Jordan River, cut off from the possession of the holy land. Taken as a symbol of heavenly realities, this Jordan can be seen as watering and inundating thirsty souls and senses next to it.

Even the following instance will not seem superfluous: Moses hears from God all the things which are written down in the laws of Leviticus; but in Deuteronomy the people become hearers of Moses and learn from him what they could not hear from God. Therefore, as a "second law," it is called Deuteronomy [Deut. 5:1ff.]. For a number of readers this will mean that at the cessation of the first law given by Moses, a second body of law seems to have emerged which Moses transmitted personally to Joshua, his successor. Joshua is generally believed to represent a type of our Savior whose second law, that is, the precepts of the Gospel, brings everything to perfection.

(III, 13) We must examine, however, whether perhaps this instance is not rather an indication of something else. Just as in Deuteronomy the body of law is set down more clearly and openly than in its first written form, so the advent of the Savior which he lived out in lowliness, taking upon himself the form of a servant [Phil. 2:7], may point forward to his more splendid and glorious second advent when he will come in the glory of his Father; in this advent the type of Deuteronomy will find its fulfillment, when all the saints will live by the laws of that eternal gospel in the kingdom of heaven. And just as in his present coming he fulfilled the law which displays a shadow of the good things to come [Heb. 10:1], so the shadow of this coming will find its fulfillment and perfection in that glorious (second) advent. For the prophet said about him: "The breath of our face is Christ the Lord of whom we said: Under his shadow we shall live among the nations" [Lam. 4:20]; this will occur at the time when he will transfer all the saints in a more worthy manner from the temporal gospel to the "eternal gospel" according to the designation used by John in his Revelation [Rev. 14:6].

(Jerome) We may even want to extend our inquiry to the passion of our Lord and Savior. It may be daring and audacious to seek his passion in heaven. But if there are "spiritual hosts of wickedness in the heavenly places" [Eph. 6:12] and we are not ashamed to confess the cross of the Lord as bringing destruction upon those powers which he destroyed by his passion, why should we be afraid to assume something similar at the consummation of the ages in the higher regions so that nations of all regions will be saved by his passion?

(Rufinus) (III, 14) In considering all of this, however, it should be sufficient for us to conform our understanding to the rule of piety and to think of the words of the Holy Spirit without expecting the brilliance of a well-composed speech reflecting a rhetoric devised by human frailty. As it is written: "All the glory of the king is within" [Ps. 44:14, LXX], and the treasure of divine meanings remains enshrined in the frail vessel of the humble letter. Should someone be more curious and seek an explanation of specific details, let him come and listen with us to Paul as he scrutinizes the depths of divine wisdom and knowledge with the help of the Holy Spirit who "searches even the depths of God"; still unable to reach the goal and to arrive at innermost knowledge, if I may say so, he cries out in desperation and utter amazement: "O the depth of the riches and wisdom and knowledge of God!" [Rom. 11:33]. One can gather from his own words how deeply he despaired of perfect com-

prehension: "How unsearchable are his judgments and how inscrutable his ways!" Paul did not say that it is difficult to search out the judgments of God but that it is impossible; he did not say that God's ways are difficult to fathom but that they cannot be fathomed at all. One may move ahead in one's search and make progress by an ever more intense effort. One may have the assistance of the grace of God enlightening one's mind. Still, one cannot arrive at the perfect goal, reaching that which is sought. No created mind has the ability to comprehend completely. But as our mind discovers some small part of the goal it seeks, it notices other problems which call out for investigation; and when it comes to terms with them, it sees many more problems arising from them which must be explored. This is why one of the wisest, Solomon, contemplating the nature of things by wisdom, had to confess: "I said: I will become wise. But wisdom itself was far from me, farther than it had been; who will find out its profound depth?" [Eccles. 7:23–24]. There is also Isaiah who knows that the beginning of things cannot be grasped by mortal nature, not even by natures who, though they are more divine than human beings, are nevertheless themselves made or created. Knowing that none of them can grasp either beginning or end, he issues the challenge: "Tell us the former things, what they were, and we shall know that you are gods; announce the last things, what they are; then we will see that you are gods!" [Isa. 41:22–23].

Concerning this topic, a Hebrew scholar taught me the following tradition: Since no one except the Lord Jesus Christ alone and the Holy Spirit can comprehend the beginning and the end of all things, therefore Isaiah, he said, made the point through the image of his vision that there are just two seraphim: with two wings they cover the face of God, with two they cover his feet, and with two they fly, each calling out to the other and saying: "Holy, holy, holy, Lord Sabaoth; the whole earth is full of your glory" [Isa. 6:2–3]. Now, since these two seraphim alone hold their wings over the face of God and over his feet, we must dare to state that neither the hosts of holy angels, nor the holy thrones, dominions, principalities, or powers can fully know the beginning of all things and the ends of the universe.

Still, we must understand that these holy spirits and powers which we have listed are indeed very close to the beginnings and attain a measure of knowledge which others are unable to reach. Yet however much these powers may have learned through the revelation of the Son of God and of the Holy Spirit—indeed they are able to know a great deal, the higher powers even far more than the lower ones—it is still impossible for them to comprehend everything, since it is written: "Most of God's works remain in secret" [Sir. 16:21].

One would wish, therefore, that everyone might do whatever is in his power always to strain forward to that which lies ahead, forgetting what lies behind [Phil. 3:13]. Everyone should strive for better deeds as well as purer insight and understanding through Jesus Christ our Savior, to whom belongs glory forever.

(III, 15) Therefore, everyone who cares about truth should be not much concerned about names and words, since individual nations have their different linguistic usage. One should pay more attention to the meaning than to the words by which meaning is expressed, especially in such weighty and difficult matters. This applies, for instance, when the question is asked whether there is a substance in which neither color, nor shape, nor touch, nor size can be distinguished, a substance perceptible only to the mind which everyone calls as he pleases. The Greeks call it *asōmaton,* that is, incorporeal, but holy Scripture uses the term invisible. The Apostle declares that God is invisible since he calls Christ "the image of the invisible God" [Col. 1:15]. But he also says that through Christ "all things were created, visible and invisible" [Col. 1:16]; this amounts to an affirmation that even among creatures there are some substances which, by the property of their own nature, are invisible. But although they are not themselves corporeal, they use bodies despite their superiority over the corporeal substance. When it comes to the substance of that Trinity, however, which is the first principle and cause of everything, since from it and through it and in it are all things [cf. Rom. 11:36], one must believe that it is neither a body nor in a body but wholly incorporeal.

What we have said here briefly, by way of digression but following the logic of the subject matter, may in itself suffice to show that there are realities whose meaning cannot be properly expressed by any words of human language; it is affirmed by a simpler act of intellectual comprehension rather than by any properties words may have. This truth must also determine our understanding of the divine writings. What they say should not be judged by the lowliness of the verbal expression but by the divinity of the Holy Spirit who inspired their composition.

VI.

CHRISTIAN ALLEGORIZATIONS

(*Fragment 1*)   [From Matthew]

(Matt. 19:24) It is easier for a camel to go through the eye of a
needle than for a rich man (to enter) the kingdom of
heaven.
    The camel is Judas;
    the needle's eye, salvation;
    the rich man, the devil.

(Matt. 13:33) The kingdom of heaven is like leaven which a
woman took and hid in three measures of meal.
    The leaven is the Spirit;
    the woman, Mary;
    the meal, the body;
    . . . . . Christ;
    the three measures, the tomb.

From John

(John 2:1) On the third day there was a marriage at Cana in
Galilee.
    The day is Christ;
    the third, faith;
    the wedding, the calling of the Gentiles;
    Cana, the church.

From Luke

(Luke 3:8) God is able to raise up children for Abraham even
from these stones.

The stones are the Gentiles;
the children, the apostles;
Abraham, Christ.

From Proverbs

(Prov. 13:14) The law of the wise is a fountain of life.
The law is the proclamation;
the wise man, Paul;
the fountain of life, Christ.

From the Wisdom of Sirach [?]

(Prov. 14:1) Wise women built their houses.
The wise women are the churches;
the houses, the holy fathers.

(Prov. 10:1) A wise son makes a glad father, but a foolish son is
a sorrow to his mother.
The wise son is Paul;
the father, the Savior;
the foolish, Judas;
the mother, the church.

(Prov. 14:16) A wise man is cautious and turns away from evil.
The wise man (is) Paul;
After his conversion, he fled the . . . .

(Prov. 15:21) A man of understanding walks aright.
The man of understanding is Paul;
the right one, Christ.

(Prov. 16:2) All the works of the humble man are manifest
before God, but the wicked perish on the evil day.
The humble man is Paul;
the wicked, the Jews.

(Prov. 15:7) The lips of the wise are devoted to perception.
The lips are the prophets;
the wise, the apostles;
perception, Christ.

(Prov. 14:7) The weapons of knowledge are wise lips.
The weapons are the apostles;
the lips, Christ;
wise, the gospels.

From Proverbs

(Prov. 15:2) The tongue of wise men understands beautiful things.
> The tongue is Peter;
> the wise men, the apostles;
> Peter understands beautiful things, for
> he said: You are the Son of God.

(Prov. 15:7) The lips of the wise are devoted to perception.
> The lips are the prophets;
> the wise, the apostles;
> perception, Christ.

(Prov. 16:22) The fountain of life is understanding. . . .
> . . . .

(Prov. 16:13) Righteous lips are pleasing to the king.
> The king is Christ;
> the righteous lips, the apostles.

(Prov. 16:26) A man troubles himself in his labors and drives out his perdition.
> The man is Christ;
> the labors, the afflictions which he underwent;
> the perdition, sin.

(Prov. 16:32) He who controls his anger is better (than he who takes a city). . . .
> . . . .

VII.

Diodore of Tarsus

COMMENTARY ON THE PSALMS, PROLOGUE

According to the blessed Paul, "all Scripture is inspired by God and profitable for teaching, for reproof, for correction, for training in righteousness" [2 Tim. 3:16]. Indeed, Scripture teaches what is useful, exposes what is sinful, corrects what is deficient, and thus it completes the perfect human being; for Paul adds: "that the man of God may be complete, equipped for every good work" [v. 17]. Certainly, one would not be mistaken in concluding that all this praise of holy Scripture is also applicable to the book of holy psalms. This book teaches righteousness in a gentle and suitable manner to those who are willing to learn; it reproves kindly and without harshness those who are too presumptuous; it corrects whatever regrettable mistakes we make unwittingly or even deliberately.

This understanding, however, does not impress itself upon us in the same way when we are just chanting the psalms as when we find ourselves in those very same situations which suggest to us our need for the psalms. Of course, those who need only the psalms of thanksgiving because life has been exceedingly kind to them are very fortunate. But we are human, and it is impossible for us not to experience difficulties and encounter the forces of necessity rising both from without and from within ourselves. Thus, when our souls find in the psalms the most ready formulation of the concerns they wish to bring before God, they recognize them as a wonderfully appropriate remedy. For the Holy Spirit anticipated all kinds of human situations, setting forth through the most blessed David the proper words for our sufferings through which the afflicted may find healing. Thus, whatever we treat lightly when merely chanting the psalms and grasp only superficially at first, we come to understand and own when we encounter the forces of necessity and affliction. In an almost natural fashion the very wound in us attracts the proper remedy, and the remedy adapts itself in turn, expressing the corresponding sentiment.

Therefore, I thought it might be proper for me to offer a concise exposition of the subjects of this very necessary part of Scripture, I mean the psalms, as I myself have received it: an exposition of the arguments as they fit the psalms individually, and an explanation of their plain text. In this way, the brothers should find no occasion to be carried away by the words when they chant, or to have their minds occupied with other things because they do not understand the meaning. Rather, grasping the logical coherence of the words, they should be able to "sing intelligently" as it is written [Ps. 44:8b, LXX], from the depth of their mind, not from shallow sentiments or just with the tip of their tongues.

Now the subject matter of the psalter in general is divided into two categories: ethical and doctrinal. In addition, the ethical category has the following subdivisions: Some of the psalms correct the moral behavior of the individual, others of the Jewish people only, still others of all human beings in general. Our detailed commentary will specify to which group each psalm belongs. It also will point out two subcategories within the doctrinal subject matter. Some psalms argue against the idea that all beings are self-moved, others against the claim that not all beings are subject to divine providence. Now the advocate of the opinion that they are self-moved automatically assumes that they are not subject to divine providence either. But the skeptic who denies that they are subject to divine providence does not necessarily imply that they are also self-moved. He may, in fact, confess a creator of the universe under whatever name he gives him; but he will either strip him of providence altogether or restrict his providence to celestial phenomena. Against such opinions, the psalms present their proofs that all being has one and the same God and creator, that his providence extends even to the smallest things, and that nothing which owes him its existence escapes his continuing providence. It is not true that God was concerned only about his power to create small and insignificant things but cared little about exercising providence over his weakest creatures; or that, because of the absolute pre-eminence of his own worth, he relinquished his concern for things whose creator he did not disdain to be. In following our detailed commentary, the reader will certainly recognize this category of psalms.

Still another subject appears in the psalms: the Babylonian captivity. Here again we have a subdivision, or rather, several subdivisions. Some of these psalms seem to be spoken by people facing deportation, others by people already in captivity, others by people hoping to return, still others by people who have returned. There are also other psalms describing past events in which, for the benefit of later generations, the prophet recalls what happened in Egypt and in the desert. There are even Maccabean psalms, some spoken in the person of specific individuals such as Onias and leaders like him; others in the collective person of all Israelites enduring the sufferings of that time. There are still other psalms which fit Jeremiah and Ezekiel specifically. Even these, however, belong to the predictive genre. For some of them reveal misfortunes which were going to come upon the nation on account of its numerous sins; some announce the incredible wonders which were to follow upon such misfortunes. There is a great variety in their composition corresponding to the variety of those future events, for the Holy Spirit was providing a remedy in advance for those who suffered.

But we do not want to bore our readers who wish to get to the detailed commentary on individual psalms by keeping them busy with this great variety of subjects. Therefore, let us stop here and move on to the texts themselves. We only want to remind the brothers of one more preliminary point, though they know it already: The entire prophetic genre is subject to the threefold division into future, present, and past. For even Moses' account of the events concerning Adam and of the very early times from the beginning on is prophecy. By the same token, the disclosure of hidden things in the present is equally prophetic; an example is Peter's knowledge of the theft of Ananias and Sapphira [Acts 5:1–11]. Most prominent, however, is the prophecy predicting future events, sometimes many generations in advance. Thus, the prophets predicted the coming of Christ, and the apostles the acceptance of the Christian faith by the Gentiles and its rejection by the Jews.

Let us begin now, following the order of items in the Book of Psalms itself, not the order of events which they reflect. For the psalms are not arranged in chronological order but in the order of their discovery. Numerous psalms will provide evidence of this, most strikingly a comparison of the inscription of Psalm 3, "A Psalm of David when he fled from the face of his son Absalom," with the inscription of Psalm 143, "A song against Goliath." Who does not know that the Goliath episode occurred much earlier than the events concerning Absalom? The psalms suffered much displacement because the book was accidentally lost during the Babylonian captivity. Afterwards, about the time of Ezra, it was rediscovered, though not the whole book at once but piecemeal—one, two, or perhaps three psalms at a time. These were then reassembled in the order in which they were found, not as they were arranged originally. Hence, even the inscriptions are mostly incorrect; more often than not, the collectors tried to guess the context of the psalms they found but did not treat them according to a scholarly method.

Nevertheless, with the help of God, we shall attempt an explanation even of these errors as far as this is possible. We will not shrink from the truth but will expound it according to the historical substance (*historia*) and the plain literal sense (*lexis*). At the same time, we will not disparage anagogy and the higher *theōria*. For history is not opposed to *theōria*. On the contrary, it proves to be the foundation and the basis of the higher senses. One thing is to be watched, however: *theōria* must never be understood as doing away with the underlying sense; it would then be no longer *theōria* but allegory. For wherever anything else is said apart from the foundational sense, we have not *theōria* but allegory. Even the apostle did not discard history at any point although he could introduce *theōria* and call it allegory [cf. Gal. 4:28]. He was not ignorant of the term but was teaching us that, if the term "allegory" is judged by its conceptual content, it must be taken in the sense of *theōria,* not violating in any way the nature of the historical substance. But those who pretend to "improve" Scripture and who are wise in their own conceit have introduced allegory because they are careless about the historical substance, or they simply abuse it. They follow not the apostle's intention but their own vain imagination, forcing the reader to take one thing for another. Thus they read "demon" for abyss, "devil" for dragon, and so on. I stop here so that I will not be compelled to talk foolishly myself in order to refute foolishness.

While repudiating this (kind of interpretation) once and for all, we are not prevented from "theorizing" responsibly and from lifting the conceptual content into higher anagogy. We may compare, for example, Cain and Abel to the Jewish synagogue and the church; we may attempt to show that like Cain's sacrifice the Jewish synagogue was rejected, while the offerings of the church are being well received as was Abel's offering at that time; we may interpret the unblemished sacrificial lamb required by the law as the Lord. This method neither sets aside history nor repudiates *theōria.* Rather, as a realistic, middle-of-the-road approach which takes into account both history and *theōria,* it frees us, on the one hand, from a Hellenism which says one thing for another and introduces foreign subject matter; on the other hand, it does not yield to Judaism and choke us by forcing us to treat the literal reading of the text as the only one worthy of attention and honor, while not allowing the exploration of a higher sense beyond the letter also. In summary, this is what the person approaching the interpretation of the divine psalms ought to know.

VIII.

Diodore of Tarsus

PREFACE TO THE COMMENTARY
ON PSALM 118

In any approach to holy Scripture, the literal reading of the text reveals some truths while the discovery of other truths requires the application of *theōria*. Now, given the vast difference between *historia* and *theōria*, allegory and figuration (*tropologia*) or parable (*parabolē*), the interpreter must classify and determine each figurative expression with care and precision so that the reader can see what is history and what is *theōria*, and draw his conclusions accordingly.

Above all, one must keep in mind one point which I have stated very clearly in my prologue to the psalter: Holy Scripture knows the term "allegory" but not its application. Even the blessed Paul uses the term: "This is said by way of allegory, for they are two covenants" [Gal. 4:25]. But his use of the word and his application is different from that of the Greeks.

The Greeks speak of allegory when something is understood in one way but said in another. Since one or two examples must be mentioned for the sake of clarity, let me give an example. The Greeks say that Zeus, changing himself into a bull, seized Europa and carried her across the sea to foreign places. This story is not understood as it reads but is taken to mean that Europa was carried across the sea having boarded a ship with a bull as figurehead. A real bull could not possibly swim such a distance across the ocean. This is allegory. Or another example: Zeus called Hera his sister and his wife. The plain text implies that Zeus had intercourse with his sister Hera so that the same person was both his wife and his sister. This is what the letter suggests; but the Greeks allegorize it to mean that, when ether, a fiery element, mingles with air, it produces a certain mixture which influences events on earth. Now, since air adjoins ether, the text calls these elements brother and sister because of their vicinity, but husband and wife because of their mixture. Of such kind are the allegories of the Greeks. The above examples should suffice lest, with all this allegory, I as an interpreter fall into foolishness myself as I mentioned earlier.

Holy Scripture does not speak of allegory in this way. In what way then does it speak? Let me explain briefly. Scripture does not repudiate in any way the underlying prior history but "theorizes," that is, it develops a higher vision (*theōria*) of other but similar events in addition, without abrogating history. As a test case, let us consider the very text of the apostle quoted above. This will be the most effective demonstration of our affirmation that the apostle means this *theōria* when he speaks of allegory. Based on the historical account of Isaac and Ishmael and their mothers, I mean Sarah and Hagar, Paul develops the higher *theōria* in the following way: He understands Hagar as Mount Sinai but Isaac's mother as the free Jerusalem, the future mother of all believers. The fact that the apostle "theorizes" in this way does not mean that he repudiates the historical account. For who could persuade him to say that the story of Hagar and Sarah was untrue? With the historical account as his firm foundation, he develops his *theōria* on top of it; he understands the underlying facts as events on a higher level. It is this developed *theōria* which the apostle calls allegory. As we said, he is aware of the term "allegory" but does not at all accept its application. I have expressed this conviction in my prologue to the psalter already, but for the sake of clarity it bears repetition here.

Figuration (*tropologia*) is present when, in describing an event, the prophet turns words with an obvious meaning into an expanded illustration of what he is saying. The figurative expression is then clarified by the continuation of the text. For instance, David says of the people: "You (God) removed a vine from Egypt" [Ps. 79:9, LXX]; then, having identified the people with the vine and leaving no doubt by adding, "you drove away the nations and transplanted it," he continues describing the people as if he were speaking of a vine. He mentions that the vine grew and unfolded its shoots [vv. 10–12]; he asks: "Why have you broken down its hedge so that all who pass by on their way pick its fruits?" [v. 13] and then adds: "A wild boar from the thicket has laid it waste" [v. 14]. Now it is quite clear that this is a covert allusion to Antiochus Epiphanes who brought great harm upon the Maccabees, yet at the same time the prophet continues his figure; speaking of the people as a vine, he calls Antiochus a wild boar who tramples down the vine. Isaiah also uses this figure of the people, calling them a vineyard and saying: "My friend had a vineyard on the hillside on fertile ground. I surrounded it with a wall and fenced it in," and so on [Isa. 5:1–2]. At the very end, clarifying the figurative character of the account, or rather of his prophecy, he adds: "For the vineyard of the Lord of hosts is the house of Israel, and the man of Judah is his beloved plantation. I waited for him to execute judgment but he acted lawlessly; instead of righteousness there was an outcry" [v. 7]. This is figuration (*tropologia*).

A parabolic expression (*parabolē*) is easy to recognize when it follows upon an introductory "like" or "as." To give some examples: "Like water I am poured out and all my bones are scattered" [Ps. 21:15, LXX]; or "I have become to them like a dead abomination" [Ps. 37:2, LXX, *varia lectio*]. There are many instances which follow this pattern. Often, however, Scripture speaks parabolically even without this introduction. It says, for instance: "You have made my arm a brazen bow" [Ps. 17:35, LXX] instead of "like a brazen bow"; or: "And when Abraham looked up with his eyes, he saw three men" [Gen. 18:2] instead of "something resembling three men." In these cases, Scripture formulates parables by way of ellipsis, omitting the word "like." Frequently, Scripture also calls a narrative or a teaching "parable," for instance, when we read: "I will open my mouth in a parable, I will utter problems from the beginning" [Ps. 77:2, LXX]. Here the author's teaching, or at least the narrative, is called a parable. Actually, the parable itself may sometimes be called a "problem." Thus, it is even possible to speak of a problem as an "enigma": Samson proposed such a "problem" to the Philistines, or rather to the Palestinians—the Philistines are in fact the Palestinians—by saying: "Out of the eater came forth food and out of the strong one came forth sweetness" [Judg. 14:14]. He would have defeated the Palestinians had he not been betrayed, being unable to resist his lust for women, so that his sophisticated problem ended up being foolishness. This is the language of parable and problem, sometimes introduced by "like" or "as," sometimes not.

One would probably classify much of the material in the books of Moses as enigmas (*ainigmata*) rather than allegories. When the author writes: "The serpent said to the woman"; "the woman said to the serpent"; "God said to the serpent," we have enigmas. Not that there was no serpent; indeed there was a serpent, but the devil acted through it. Moses speaks of the serpent as the visible animal but under this cover hints at the devil in a hidden way. If this was allegory, only the word "serpent" should be there as we explained earlier. The truth is that there was both a reality and an enigma. The reality was the serpent but, since a serpent is by nature irrational and yet was speaking, it is obvious that it spoke empowered by the devil. (Christ), who has the authority to reveal mysteries and enigmas, points this out in the gospels when he says of the devil: "He was a murderer from the beginning and has not stood in the truth . . . , for he is a liar and the father of it" [John 8:44]. This phrase, "and the father of it," is very apt, for the devil was the first one to lie as well as the one who begot lying. Therefore Christ adds, "and the father of it," instead of saying, "the lie in person." Now the Lord was able to clarify enigmas; the prophets and apostles could only report realities. Therefore, both Moses and the Apostle Paul said "serpent." The latter puts it this way: "I fear lest, as the serpent seduced Eve by its guile, so your minds may be corrupted" [2 Cor. 11:3]; here he also hints at the devil by mentioning the serpent. The serpent is not a rational animal for him but points enigmatically to the devil acting through it. Scheming is not the action of an irrational animal but of a rational being. Our brief remarks here must suffice on the topic of these figurative expressions. We have mentioned only a few points among many, leaving room for industrious scholars to make further points on the basis of similar examples.

In contrast, history (*historia*) is the pure account of an actual event of the past. It is authentic if it is not interwoven with the speaker's reflections, extraneous episodes, characterizations or fictitious speeches as is, for example, the story of Job. A plain, clear, and concise historical account does not weary the reader with reflections of the author and long characterizations.

Let this be enough on this mode of expression. But since, by the grace of God, I intend to interpret the 118th psalm, I had to discuss in detail the above-mentioned modes of expression, as this psalm contains many of them. Therefore, I had to give my readers a clear statement about them in the preface already in order to alert them to the fact that some parts of the psalms are meant to be taken literally while others are figurative expressions, parables, or enigmas. What is emphatically not present is allegory. Of course, some interpreters have fancied that it is. They brush aside any historical understanding, introduce foolish fables of their own making in place of the text, and burden their readers' ears, leaving their minds devoid of pious thoughts. If they said that, being an utterance of God, this psalm accompanies generations of human beings, conforming itself to events both actual and on a higher plane, their interpretation would be quite correct. I am attempting to say something like this: In predicting future events, the prophets adapted their words both to the time in which they were speaking and to later times. Their words sounded hyperbolic in their contemporary setting but were entirely fitting and consistent at the time when the prophecies were fulfilled. For the sake of clarity there is nothing wrong with stressing this point more than once.

Historically, Psalm 29 was spoken by Hezekiah at the occasion of his deliverance from an illness and from the threat of war with the Assyrians [2 Kings 19–20]. These are his words after he was delivered from those ills: "I will extol you, O Lord, for you have protected me and have not let my foes rejoice over me. O Lord, my God, I cried to you and you have healed me. O Lord, you have brought up my soul from Hades, you have rescued me from those who go down to the pit" [Ps.29: 1–3, LXX]. Now these words did fit Hezekiah when he was delivered from his ills; but they also fit all human beings when they obtain the promised resurrection. For at that moment it will be timely for everyone to say to God what Hezekiah said: "I will extol you, O Lord, for you have protected me and have not let my foes rejoice over me." In Hezekiah's case, the foes were the Assyrians and those who rejoiced over his illness; the primary foes of all human beings are physical sufferings, death itself, and the devil, the whole range of experiences connected with mortality. Again, when the psalm continues: "O Lord, my God, I cried to you and you have healed me; Lord, you have brought up my soul from Hades," Hezekiah seems to have used hyperbole to describe his own situation; he was not actually rescued from Hades but from circumstances comparable to Hades on account of his very serious illness. But what sounded hyperbolical at that time, "you have brought up my soul from Hades," will fit his situation much more precisely when he rises from the dead. The same applies to the following verse: "You have rescued me from those who go down to the pit." It is quite clear that by the pit the author means death, but when he first uttered these words, they were used hyperbolically. When he actually rises from the dead, the former hyperbole will come true; the events themselves will have moved in the direction of the formerly hyperbolic expression. One will find more or less all utterances of the saints to be of this kind when one observes how they are made to fit the events of their own time but are also adapted to the events of the future. For this is the grace of the Spirit who gives eternal and imperishable gifts to human beings; I am speaking of the divine words which are capable of being adapted to every moment in time, down to the final perfection of human beings.

In the same way, Psalm 84 was pronounced in the person of those Israelites who had returned from Babylon. It says: "Lord, you were favorable to your land, you have brought back the captivity of Jacob; you forgave your people their iniquity," and so on [Ps. 84:1–2, LXX]. These words were certainly fitting at the time of Israel's return; but they will be even more suitable at the resurrection when, freed from our mortality, we shall be liberated from all sins even more truly. Now if one understands Psalm 118 in this way, namely, as fitting (the circumstances) of those who first uttered it as well as those who come after them, one is entirely correct. But this is not a case of allegory; rather, it is a statement adaptable to many situations according to the grace of him who gives it power. This great, rich, and beautiful psalm was pronounced in the person of the saints in Babylon who were longing to return to Jerusalem on account of the divine laws and the holy mysteries celebrated there, and who were emboldened to make such petitions by their pious lives. A man caught up in sin cannot pray for all his wishes except perhaps for deliverance from his ills; his conscience does not allow him to pray for greater gifts because it means sufficient grace for him if he is set free from his present ills. Therefore, the prayer of great and more saintly people is supported by lives accompanied by virtue. It is their virtues which allow them to make their request boldly.

Now, if this is the subject of the psalm and someone says that Psalm 118 fits all saints everywhere and that one should always pray to God for the general resurrection, as the exiles in Babylon prayed for their return to Jerusalem, this is no violation of propriety. Being so rich and lavish, the psalm adapted itself readily to the exiles in Babylon for their request and prayer, but it adapts itself even more precisely to those who fervently long for the general resurrection. Now the understanding of such a *theōria* must be left to those endowed with a fuller charism. For the purpose of our exposition, let us concentrate on the historical prayer of the saints, the prayer about Jerusalem. But if anyone should doubt that there were saints in that captivity, he is totally mistaken. Yes, there were many saints; some of them were famous, others turned to the Lord humble and unknown, suffering no harm by being unknown to the world. Paul says about them: "Many went about in skins of sheep and goats, destitute, afflicted, ill-treated," and adds: "of whom the world was not worthy" [Heb. 11:37–38]. He has added this clause so that no one may wonder why they were not known. There was no harm in being unknown, but the world proved unworthy of knowing such saints. There were, however, famous people also—I mean in Babylon—outstanding in piety and virtue, men such as Daniel and the three youths, Ezekiel, Zerubbabel, Jesus son of Jozadak, Ezra, and others like them. But this psalm is on the lips of all saints in captivity or on the way home. They all teach us that it is the practice of virtue and piety above all which has the strength and power to render our prayers effective before God. Thus, David the prophet begins the psalm with these words: "Blessed are those who are blameless in their way," and so on [Ps. 118:1, LXX].

IX

Theodore of Mopsuestia

COMMENTARY ON GALATIANS 4:22-31

It is written that Abraham had two sons, one by a slave woman and one by a free woman. But the son of the slave woman was born according to the flesh, the son of the free woman by virtue of a promise. [Gal. 4:22–23]

Paul pointed out earlier that the law can have nothing in common with the promises because the law demands the hearer's obedience, while the promise proves the giver's generosity. He was eager, however, to establish the principle of grace firmly throughout. Therefore, he mentioned faith and the promises in one breath with those benefits we hope to obtain. Over against all this he placed the law, which seems to offer righteousness almost as an automatic result when it promises to offer these benefits to those who fulfill the law's demands first. But it defrauds many—virtually all, to be more precise—because those who strive to fulfill the law find it impossible to do so. Paul therefore stresses very much that the righteousness coming through grace is better than the righteousness coming from the law; God offers it in his generosity and no one is excluded because of his natural infirmity. He now repeats the same point, which he had already made in the preceding section, using a comparison from the Abraham story—that Abraham had two sons, one of them born following the course of nature, the other through grace. "For it is written that Abraham had two sons, one by a slave woman and one by a free woman. But the son of the slave woman was born according to the flesh" [Gal. 4:22]. This means he was born in the natural order. Paul uses the term, "according to the flesh," since all flesh takes part in a birth according to nature. Ishmael also was born in the natural order of the flesh both with regard to Abraham and with regard to Hagar. On the other hand, the son of the free woman was born according to the promise, that is, according to grace, for all promises are normally made by grace. If one follows the order of nature, Isaac cannot be said to have been born at all because Sarah was unable to give birth for two reasons: she suffered from sterility, and she was too old for childbirth. Even Abraham was of a quite advanced age. But Isaac was born against all hope and against the order of nature by virtue of the power and generosity of the giver of the promise alone. Thus, having rehearsed the Abraham story as one reads it in the divine Scriptures and at the same time wishing to make clear why he is using it, Paul adds: "This is said by way of allegory" [v. 24].

There are people who take great pains to twist the senses of the divine Scriptures and make everything written therein serve their own ends. They dream up some silly fables in their own heads and give their folly the name of allegory. They (mis)use the apostle's term as a blank authorization to abolish all meanings of divine Scripture. They make it a point to use the same expression as the apostle, "by way of allegory," but fail to understand the great difference between that which they say and what the apostle says here. For the apostle neither does away with history nor elaborates on events that happened long ago. Rather, he states the events just as they happened and then applies the historical account of what occurred there to his own understanding. For instance, he says at one point: "She corresponds to the present Jerusalem" [v. 25], and at another: "Just as at that time he who was born according to the flesh persecuted him who was born according to the Spirit" [v. 29]. Paul gives history priority over all other considerations. Otherwise, he would not say that Hagar "corresponds to the present Jerusalem," thus acknowledging that Jerusalem does exist now. He also would not use the term "just as" if he was referring to a person he thought did not exist. For in saying "just as" he pointed to a similarity; but similarity cannot be established if the elements involved do not exist. In addition, he says "at that time." He apparently considered the temporal interval about which he was speaking to be uncertain; but the very distinction of times would be superfluous if nothing at all had happened. Now this is the apostle's way of speaking. Those people, however, turn it all into the contrary, as if the entire historical account of divine Scripture differed in no way from dreams in the night. When they start expounding divine Scripture "spiritually"— "spiritual interpretation" is the name they like to give to their folly—they claim that Adam is not Adam, paradise is not paradise, the serpent not the serpent. I should like to tell them this: If they make history serve their own ends, they will have no history left. But if this is what they do, let them tell us how they can answer questions such as these: Who was created the first human being? How did his disobedience come about? How was our death sentence introduced? Now, if they have gleaned their answers from the Scriptures, then their so-called allegory is unmasked as being foolishness, for it proves superfluous throughout. But if their assertion is true, if the biblical writings do not preserve the narrative of actual events but point to something else, something profound which requires special understanding—something "spiritual" as they would like to say, which they have discovered because they are so spiritual themselves, then what is the source of their knowledge? Whatever name they may give to their interpretation, have they been taught by divine Scripture in their speaking? Also, I shall not even mention that, if they are correct, not even the reason for the events surrounding Christ's coming will be clear. The apostle says that Christ canceled Adam's disobedience and annulled the death sentence. What were those events in the distant past to which he refers, and where did they take place, if the historical account relating them does not signify real events but something else, as those people maintain? What room is left for the apostle's words, "but I fear lest, as the serpent seduced Eve" [2 Cor. 11:3], if there was no serpent, no Eve, nor any seduction elsewhere involving Adam? In many instances the apostle clearly uses the historical account of the ancient writers as the truth and nothing but the truth. In our passage, he attempts to prove his assertion from actual events as well as from their written record, which the Jews acknowledged as factual account. This certainly was his intention from the start. But what is his point? He wishes to show that the events surrounding Christ's coming are greater than anything contained in the law, and that the righteousness to which we have access must be considered as far more glorious than that which comes through the law.

Therefore, Paul points out that there are two covenants, one through Moses, the other through Christ. He calls the covenant in Christ the resurrection promised to all of us by Christ after he had been the first to rise from the dead. We have documented this point more fully in our commentary on the Epistle to the Hebrews. It was the purpose of Moses' legislation that those to whom the law was given should live under it and thus obtain the righteousness which comes through it. This was the reason the people had to leave Egypt and settle in a remote area; shielded from any mingling with other nations, they were to be able to observe the law they were given with appropriate care. Similarly, it was the purpose and goal of Christ's coming to abolish death and to raise up all people of all times for a new existence in an immortal nature, no longer being able to sin in any way on account of the abiding presence of the Spirit's grace in them, a grace which will preserve us too from all sin. This is the true and perfect justification. Paul called both of them "covenants" for good reason because the very point which the law taught was also enjoined by the operation of grace, namely, the love of God and neighbor. Of course, the law also demanded the observance of its precepts, insisting and teaching that one must not sin in any way. But the operation of grace fulfills this teaching through the resurrection and through immortality which will be ours through the Spirit; then, guided by him, we will indeed be completely incapable of sinning.

To be sure, justification is a reality under the law as well as in Christ. But under the law it is obtained by the person who can secure it with a great deal of effort and sweat. Now this is extremely hard, in fact impossible, if the standard of strict implementation of every command is applied. For it is impossible for a human being here on earth to live entirely without sin. Such a state is acquired by grace alone. We will be able to sin no longer only when we obtain the justification coming from Christ, apart from all our effort.

Paul speaks of Hagar and Sarah. One of them gave birth according to the order of nature; the other, though unable to give birth, bore Isaac by grace. Among their sons, the one born according to grace turned out to receive much more honor. Paul mentions the two women in order to demonstrate by their comparison that even now the justification coming from Christ is far better than the other, because it is acquired by grace. Appropriately, he takes the woman giving birth in the natural order to mean justification through the law, the woman giving birth against hope justification by grace. For a conduct regulated by law is appropriate for those living in the present age; but those who are raised up and have put on incorruption do not need circumcision, the offering of sacrifices, or the observance of special days. There is, of course, a natural order, the short time span allotted to those who are born into this life, in which a conduct regulated by law seems to have its place. But grace leads to that birth which causes all who rise again to be born into the life to come; in that birth Christ's justification is most fully implemented. Thus, Paul considered the woman giving birth in the natural order as a representation of justification according to the law because, if the law has a place at all, it controls those born into this life, that is, born according to the sequence of nature. On the other hand, the woman giving birth by grace represented for him justification according to Christ, because justification is most truly implemented among those who have been raised once and for all and expect their second birth through grace against all hope. Here we have the reason for the phrase, "this is said by way of allegory." Paul used the term "allegory" as a comparison, juxtaposing events of the past and present.

Therefore, he adds: "For they are two covenants, one from Mount Sinai bearing children for slavery, which is Hagar" [v. 24]. "For they are": Paul here returns to the preceding phrase, "this is said by way of allegory," so that one must read: "What is expressed by way of allegory are the two covenants." He wants to say that by way of allegory one can liken the two covenants to those two women, Hagar and Sarah, with Hagar representing the order of the precepts of the law, for the law was given on Mount Sinai. Her children are born for slavery because those who live under the law experience precepts and law as the imposition of an order of slavery: They are punished mercilessly if they have sinned; they are praised if they observe the law in all details. It is an arduous task requiring a great deal of effort. To be kept under the law in this manner is appropriate for slaves but not for the free-born. Pointing out that this comparison with Hagar is not foreign to the Old Testament, Paul adds: "Now Hagar is Mount Sinai in Arabia; but she corresponds to the present Jerusalem which is in slavery with her children" [v. 25].

In former times, Arabia was not only the territory known by this name today but comprised the whole desert and the inhabited borderland around it, including a significant portion of Egypt. The dwelling place of the Israelites at the time of their sojourn in Egypt fell within the borders of that Arabia. The name of their area reflects this, as we learn from divine Scripture: "They dwelt in the land of Goshen in Arabia" [cf. Gen. 47:1; 45:10; 46:34]. Since Hagar was from there, Paul wished to make the point that Mount Sinai belonged to Arabia. In this way Hagar is a fitting simile for the old covenant because it was given on Mount Sinai, a place associated with the nation from which Hagar also came.

Now, when Paul says, "She corresponds to the present Jerusalem," he is speaking of Hagar (as the subject) so that the meaning is: Hagar is the equivalent of the Jerusalem which is present with us, that is, Jerusalem regarded from the vantage point of this life. This present Jerusalem offers us an order in which the laws of the old covenant are in force, in anticipation of the expected future which we also hope to share in the coming age. It is this old order which Hagar represents in contrast to Sarah. For when Paul says, "she is in slavery with her children," he is not speaking of Hagar but of the covenant given on Sinai. He wants to explain his words, "one from Mount Sinai bearing children for slavery." Her children, he says, are those living in slavery. In fact, he puts it very well by saying that she herself "is in slavery with her children." For we can certainly recognize the kind of covenant we have here, if we consider those to whom it was given. It is not perceived in its substance; it is a covenant in slavery when those who live by it experience it as slavery.

The advocates of allegory should take a good look at the phrase, "she corresponds to the present Jerusalem." Obviously, the Jerusalem which the author connects here with Hagar is not a fiction serving his own ends. Rather, Paul wants to make clear that both Jerusalems are equivalents since by signification they are one and the same. In speaking of the first covenant, the blessed Paul speaks of the second also: "But that Jerusalem which is above is free, and she is the mother of us all" [v. 26]. When using the phrase, "the Jerusalem above," the apostle is not piling up dreams like those who believe everything must be allegorized. He uses it because he reserves the term "second covenant" for the resurrection which is still expected even by those who have been raised up and hope for permission to remain in heaven, completely free from all sin. In contrast, he speaks here of "the Jerusalem which is above," thereby designating our residence in heaven inasmuch as we will dwell there living with Christ but still conducting ourselves with all diligence. He calls this celestial abode "the Jerusalem above" because the Jews dwelling in the area of Jerusalem believed they were dwelling with God; it was here that they eagerly rendered to God the worship they owed him, convinced that this place was agreeable to him because sacrifices, burnt offerings, or other ceremonies prescribed in the law could not be offered anywhere else.

"That Jerusalem which is above is free, and she is the mother of us all" [v. 26]. Paul means: When we will have attained the resurrection and see before us that glorious second birth which will allow us to dwell in heaven, we will regard this as our Jerusalem where we will all at once enjoy the fullest freedom, freed from any need to fulfill legal precepts or other such obligations. We will dwell there with great confidence because we will no longer be subject to sin. And now Paul introduces a scriptural testimony: "For it is written: Rejoice, O barren one, that dost not bear; break forth and cry out thou who art not in travail; for many are the children of the desolate, more than of her who has a husband" [v. 27, quoting Isa. 54:1]. He does not quote this verse as a prophetic utterance about the resurrection. Rather, he uses it as a testimony because it contains the word "barren," for he understands Sarah and her barrenness as pointing to the order of the second covenant. He means to say: All these blessings will come to us against hope. For we who are dead will rise again; even our number will be much larger than theirs. Joined in this second covenant, we will be far more numerous. Those who are under the law as their covenant are one nation. But we who will attain the covenant of the resurrection are children, all of us.

Therefore, Paul adds: "But we, brethren, like Isaac, are children of the promise" [v. 28]. "Like Isaac" means: Our existence will be like that of Isaac, not according to nature but according to grace. For as Isaac was born against all hope, so the resurrection is a gift of grace, not a result of nature. Paul proves the difference of the covenants from the contents of divine Scripture, demonstrating that the results of grace are much better than the results of nature. Armed with this logic, he even refers to present events: "But just as at that time he who was born according to the flesh persecuted him who was born according to the spirit, so also it is now" [v. 29]. In speaking of those living in Christ, Paul does not only use words like "faith" or "promise," but also "spirit." In fact, he uses this word very frequently as one can readily observe, for example, in Romans. For it is by participation in the spirit that we expect to receive the enjoyment of our future blessings. In a similar manner he uses the word "flesh" in speaking of those who live under the law, for the law can be useful in terms of this present life; "flesh" is his word for something transient and easy to dissolve, when he is not simply describing our (human) nature. We have documented this usage at many points in our interpretation of the Pauline epistles; our full exegesis here proves it again, at least to those who are willing to study the text very carefully. Hagar was cast out. She was the one giving birth according to the natural order and served as a type of the old covenant, because she could represent the order of those born naturally into this present life. We spoke about this earlier. "But just as at that time he who was born in the natural order persecuted him who was born through the promise, so it is now"; the defenders of the law try to drive out anything that has to do with grace. Paul said aptly, "according to the spirit," when he wanted to designate Isaac who was born according to the promise. By using the similitude of his person he wanted to place us on the opposite side (of the flesh) because we are truly called by the name of the Spirit on account of our beliefs. At this point I should like to ask my dear allegorists whether divine Scripture contains a record of Ishmael persecuting Isaac, thus signifying that there were some circumcised Jews who, at some point in very recent times, might have tried to bring back under the law those Galatians who had come to believe in Christ. Who can duly deride this (nonsense)? If nothing else, the allegorists should at least recognize that the apostle used the historical account in his narrative as a record of actual events written down as such, in order to confirm what he had said previously. Here, however, he wanted to present history in this particular image for the sake of comparison. Therefore, we see him in this instance even inventing external events which happened to his figures.

He adds somewhat inconsistently but with a grand gesture: "But what does Scripture say? Cast out the slave woman and her son, for the son of the slave woman shall not be heir with the son of the free woman" [v. 30]. Paul means: Their effort does not help them, just as it did not help Hagar at that time. For present and future have nothing in common, and legal precepts have no place in ordering our conduct in which we try to implement the pattern of the resurrection. Why then do they try so hard to bring those who believe in Christ under the custody of the law? He concludes by recapitulating, as it were, all his previous explanations: "Therefore, brethren, we are not children of the slave woman but of the free woman" [v. 31]. And once this is said, he adds an exhortation: "Stand fast in the freedom for which Christ has set us free, and do not submit again to the yoke of slavery" [Gal. 5:1].

X.

Tyconius

THE BOOK OF RULES, I–III

(*Prologue*) I thought it necessary before anything else which occurred to me to write a brief book of rules providing something like keys and windows to the secrets of the law. For there are certain mystical rules which govern the depth of the entire law and hide the treasures of truth from the sight of some people. If the logic of these rules is accepted without prejudice as we set it down here, every closed door will be opened and light will be shed on every obscurity. Guided, as it were, by these rules in paths of light, a person walking through the immense forest of prophecy may well be defended from error.

These rules are as follows:

    I.   Of the Lord and His Body
   II.   Of the Lord's Bipartite Body
  III.   Of Promises and the Law
  IV.   Of Species and Genus
   V.   Of Times
  VI.   Of Recapitulation
 VII.   Of the Devil and His Body

I. Of the Lord and His Body

(1) Reason alone discerns whether Scripture is speaking of the Lord or his Body, that is, the church. It suggests the appropriate referent by convincing argument or by the sheer power of the truth which forces itself on the reader. In other instances, Scripture seems to speak of one person only, but the fact that this person functions in different ways indicates a double mean-

ing. Thus, Isaiah says: "He bears our sins and suffers pain for us; he was wounded for our offenses, and God abandoned him for our sins," and so on [Isa. 53:4–5]. This is a passage which the confession of the whole church applies to the Lord. But Isaiah continues, speaking of the same one: "And God wants to cleanse him from the stroke and to relieve his soul from pain, to let him see the light and to fashion him in wisdom" [vv. 10–11]. Does God want to let him see the light whom he abandoned for our sins, and fashion him in wisdom who is already the light and the wisdom of God? Does this continuation not rather apply to his Body? This example shows that one can discern by reason alone the point at which the text makes the transition from the head to the body.

(2) Daniel calls the Lord "the stone hewn from the mountain" which struck the body of the kingdoms of this world and "ground it to dust." But when "the stone became a mountain and filled the whole earth," he is speaking of the Lord's Body [Dan. 2:34–35]. The Lord does not fill the world only by his power but not by the fullness of his Body, as some maintain. Such a statement is an insult to the kingdom of God and the invincible inheritance of Christ. It is painful for me even to mention it. Indeed, some claim that the mountain filling the earth is the fact that the Christian may now present his offering everywhere, while formerly sacrifice was allowed only on Mount Zion. If this were the case, it would be unnecessary to say that the stone grew into a mountain and began to fill the world by its growth. For our Lord Christ "had this glory before the world was made" [John 17:5], and since in him God's Son became man, he received "all power in heaven and on earth" [Phil. 2:11], not gradually like the stone, but all at once. The stone, however, became a large mountain by a process of growth and in growing covered the whole earth. If Christ filled the whole earth just by his power and not by his Body, there would be no point in comparing him to a stone, for power is something intangible but a stone is a tangible body. Moreover, that growth occurs in the body and not in the head is demonstrated not only by reason but is also confirmed by apostolic authority. "We grow up in all things," says the apostle, "into

him who is the head, Christ, from whom the whole body, fashioned and knit together through every joint of the system in the measure of each and every part, derives its increase to the building up of itself" [Eph. 4:15–16]. And also: "(Such a one) is not united to the head from whom the whole body, supplied and built up with joints and ligaments, attains a growth that is from God" [Col. 2:19]. What grows, therefore, is not the head. The head is the same from the very beginning. Instead, the body grows from the head.

(3) But let us return to our theme. The following passage concerns the Lord and his Body, but the correct referent must be discerned by reason: "To his angels he has given command about you, that they guard you in all your ways. Upon their hands they shall bear you up lest you dash your foot against a stone. You shall tread upon the asp and the viper; you shall trample down the lion and the dragon. Because he hopes in me, I will deliver him; I will protect him, for he knows my name. He will call upon me, and I will answer him; I am with him in distress. I will deliver him and glorify him. I will make full for him the length of days and will show him my salvation" [Ps. 90:11–16, LXX]. Tell me, did God show his salvation to the one whom he commanded angels to serve? Did he not rather show it to his Body?

Another instance: "Like a bridegroom he crowned me with a mitre; like a bride he adorned me with adornment" [Isa. 61:10]. The text speaks of one body of two sexes, the groom's and the bride's. Reason discerns what applies to the Lord and what applies to the church. The same Lord says in the Book of Revelation: "I am the bridegroom and the bride" [Rev. 22:17], and also: "They went out to meet the bridegroom and the bride" [Matt. 25:1]. Once more, Isaiah makes clear which part reason must attribute to the head and which to the body: "Thus says the Lord to the Christ, my Lord, whose right hand I grasped so that nations might listen to him" [Isa. 45:1]. This statement is followed by another which applies to the Body only: "And I will give you hidden treasures, invisible treasures I will open up for you that you may know that I am the Lord, the God of Israel, who calls you by your name for the sake of Jacob, my son, and of Israel, my chosen one" [Isa. 45:3]. Having made covenants with the fathers in order that he might be known, God opens invisible treasures to the Body of Christ, treasures which "eye has not seen or ear heard, nor have they entered into the heart of man" [1 Cor. 2:9]. "Of man"—this, of course, is said of a hardened man who is not in the Body of Christ. To the church "God revealed them through his Spirit" [v. 10]. Nevertheless, the use of reason sometimes helps to perceive these treasures more easily even though this perception occurs through the grace of God as well.

(4) In other cases such reasoning is less successful because the text can be applied correctly to both, either the Lord or his Body. In such instances the proper meaning can be perceived only by an even greater grace from God. Thus, we read in the gospel: "From now on you will see the Son of Man sitting at the right hand of the power and coming on the clouds of heaven" [Matt. 24:64]. But Scripture states elsewhere that he will be seen coming on the clouds of heaven only on the last day: "All the nations of the earth will mourn, and then they will see the Son of Man coming on the clouds of heaven" [Matt. 24:30]. Indeed, two things must happen: first, the advent of the Body, that is, the church, which is continually coming in one and the same invisible glory; then the advent of the head, that is, the Lord, in manifest glory. If the text had read: "Now you will see him coming," it would refer only to the advent of the Body; if it had read: "You will see him coming," it would refer only to the advent of the head. But it actually reads: "From now on you will see him coming," for he comes continually in his Body, through a birth and through the glory of sufferings like his. Since those who are reborn are made members of Christ, and these members constitute the Body, it is Christ himself who is coming. Birth means coming as when Scripture says: "He enlightens every man who comes into this world" [John 1:9]; or: "One generation passes and another comes" [Eccles. 1:4]; or: "As you have heard that Antichrist is coming" [1 John 2:18]. And concerning this latter body: "For if he who comes preaches another Jesus" [2 Cor. 11:4]. Therefore, when the Lord was asked for a sign of his coming, he began to speak of that coming which can be imitated in

signs and wonders by the opposing body. "Take heed," he said, "that no one leads you astray; for many will come in my name" [Matt. 24:4–5], that is, in the name of my Body. At the last coming of the Lord, however, that is, at the advent of the final consummation and open manifestation of his coming in its entirety, there will be no deceiver, as some people think. But this matter will be more fully discussed in its proper place later.

(5) Therefore, our wish to apply the mention of one person to the whole Body, to interpret, for example, the Son of Man as the church, implies no absurdity. After all, the church, that is, the children of God gathered into one Body, is called "son of God," or "one man," or even "God," as in the words of the apostle: "above all that is called God, or that is worshiped" [2 Thess. 2:4]. Here, "that is called God," means the church, and "that is worshiped," means the highest God. The apostle continues: "so that he takes his seat in the temple of God pretending to be God" [v. 5], that is, to be the church. It is like saying: "He takes his seat in the temple of God pretending to be the temple of God," or: "He takes his seat in God pretending to be God." The apostle wants to veil this understanding by using synonyms. Daniel says the following about a king of the end time: "In God will his place be glorified" [cf. Dan. 11:38], that is, made famous. This king will secretly establish something like a church in the place of the church, in the holy place; an "abomination of devastation" [Matt. 24:15] in God, that is, in the church.

(6) The Lord himself calls the whole people "bride" and "sister" [Song of Sol. 5:1]. The apostle calls it a "holy virgin" but terms the opposing body "the man of sin" [2 Cor. 11:2; 2 Thess. 2:3]. David calls the whole church "the anointed": "He showed mercy to his anointed, David and his seed forever" [Ps. 17:51, LXX], and the apostle Paul calls the Body of Christ "Christ" when he says: "For just as the body is one but has many members, and all the members of the body, though many, are one body, so also is Christ" [1 Cor. 12:12], that is, Christ's Body which is the church. And also: "I rejoice in the sufferings I bear for your sake and complete what is lacking from the afflictions of Christ" [Col. 1:24], that is, of the church. There was certainly

nothing lacking from the sufferings of Christ; rather, "it is enough for the disciple to be like his master" [Matt. 10:25]. Thus, we will take the coming of Christ to mean what each passage suggests. Likewise, we recognize that in the Book of Exodus all sons of God are one son, and all firstborn of Egypt are one firstborn, for God says: "So you shall say to Pharaoh: Thus says the Lord, Israel is my firstborn son. Hence I tell you: Let my people go that it may serve me. But you refuse to let it go. Therefore, behold I kill your firstborn son" [Exod. 4:22–23]. Also, David calls the vineyard of the Lord one son when he says: "Turn again, O God of hosts! Look down from heaven and see; visit your vineyard and perfect what your right hand has planted, what you have confirmed as a son for yourself" [Ps. 79:15–16, LXX].

(7) The apostle gives the name "Son of God" to one who is merely mingled with the Son of God: "Paul, a servant of Jesus Christ, called to be an apostle, set apart for the gospel of God which he promised beforehand through his prophets in the holy Scriptures, the gospel concerning his Son who was born to him of the seed of David according to the flesh, who was the predestined Son of God in power according to the spirit of holiness by the resurrection from the dead of our Lord Jesus Christ" [Rom. 1:1–4]. If the text simply read: "the gospel concerning his Son, by the resurrection from the dead," it would refer to one son only. But it reads: "the gospel concerning his Son, by the resurrection from the dead of our Lord Jesus Christ." The phrase, "who was made Son of God by the resurrection of Christ," is explained more fully by the preceding words: "concerning his Son who was born to him of the seed of David according to the flesh, who was the predestined Son of God." For our Lord, being himself God and coequal with the Father, is not "the predestined Son of God," gaining his sonship through his birth. Rather, he is the one to whom God said at his baptism, as Luke tells us: "You are my Son, today I have begotten you" [cf. Luke 3:22]. The one "born of the seed of David" is mingled with the "principal spirit" [Ps. 50:14, LXX] and was made "Son of God by the resurrection of our Lord Jesus Christ," that means, when in Christ the seed of David rises up. He is not that other

one of whom David said: "Thus says the Lord to my Lord" [Ps. 109:1, LXX]. The two were made one flesh. "The word was made flesh" [John 1:14], and the flesh was made God, for "we are born not of blood but of God" [v. 13]. The apostle writes: "The two shall become one flesh. This is a great mystery; I mean it in reference to Christ and the Church" [Eph. 5:31-32]. God promised Abraham one seed; as many as would be mingled with Christ, there would be one person in Christ as the apostle himself says: "You are all one (*unus*) in Christ Jesus. But if you are one in Christ Jesus, you are Abraham's seed and heirs according to the promise" [Gal. 3:28-29]. Now there is a difference between "you are one" (*unum*) and "you are one person" (*unus*). When one person is mingled with another in (an act of) will, they are one, as the Lord says: "I and the Father are one (*unum*)" [John 10:30]. When they are also mingled in body, however, and are joined into one flesh, the two are one person (*unus*).

(8) In its head, therefore, the Body is the Son of God, and in his Body God is the Son of Man who comes daily through a birth and "grows into God's holy temple" [Eph. 2:21]. Now the temple itself is bipartite. Its second part, though built of large stones, suffers destruction; in it, "not one stone will be left upon the other" [Matt. 24:2]. We must beware of its continual coming until the church departs from its midst.

II. Of the Lord's Bipartite Body

(1) The rule about the bipartite body of the Lord is of the utmost necessity. We must investigate it all the more carefully and must keep it constantly before our eyes when reading Scripture. Now just as reason alone perceives the transition from the head to the body, as I pointed out above, so it is with the transitions from one part of the body to another, from right to left or from left to right, as the title of our present chapter indicates.

(2) When the Lord says to one body: "Invisible treasures I will open up for you that you may know that I am the Lord, and I will adopt you," and then continues: "But you did not recognize me, that I am God and there is no God beside me, and you did not know me" [Isa. 45:3-4], do the two statements, though

they are addressed to one body, actually refer to the same entity: "Invisible treasures I will open up for you that you may recognize that I am God, for the sake of my servant Jacob," and: "But you did not recognize me"? Did Jacob not receive what God had promised? Do the two verbs even refer to the same action: "You did not recognize me," and "You did not know me"? "You did not know" can only be said to someone who now does know, but "you did not recognize" is addressed to someone who, though he should have recognized (God) and seems to belong to the same body, "draws near to God with his lips only, while his heart is far from him" [Isa. 29:13]. To such a person God can say: "But you did not recognize me."

(3) Here is another instance: "I will lead the blind on a journey they do not know; they shall walk in paths they do not know, and I will turn darkness into light for them and will make the crooked straight. What I have said, I will do for them, and I will not forsake them. But they turned back" [Isa. 42:16–17]. Did the very ones of whom he said, "I will not forsake them," all turn back? Was it not just part of them?

(4) Again, the Lord says to Jacob: "Fear not, for I am with you; from the East I will bring back your seed, and from the West I will gather you. I will say to the North: Bring back! and to the South: Do not withhold! Bring back my sons from a distant land and my daughters from the ends of the earth, everyone over whom my name has been pronounced! For in my glory I created (this seed), formed and made him; but I brought forth a blind people; their eyes are blind, and their ears are deaf" [Isa. 43:5–8]. Are the very people whom he created for his glory also blind and deaf?

Or: "Your forefathers and their princes did evil to me; your princes defiled my sanctuary so that I left Jacob to perish and Israel to be cursed. Now, hear me, my son Jacob; Israel whom I have chosen!" [Isa. 43:27—44:1]. God makes it clear that he "left to perish and to be cursed" only the Jacob and the Israel whom he had *not* chosen.

(5) Or: "I formed you as my son; you are mine, O Israel, do not forget me! For behold, I have taken away your iniquities like a cloud and your sins like a storm cloud. Return to me, and I will

redeem you!" [Isa. 44:21–22]. Does he say "return to me" to the same person whose sins he took away, to the one whom he assures: "you are mine," and whom he reminds not to forget him? Are anyone's sins taken away before he returns?

Or: "I know that you will surely be rejected. For the sake of my name I will show you my excellence and will cause my magnificence to rise over you" [Isa. 48:8–9]. Is he showing his excellence and displaying his magnificence to the reprobate?

(6) Or: "Not an elder, nor an angel, but the Lord himself saved them, because he loved them and forgave them; he himself redeemed them and adopted them and exalted them throughout all the days of this age. But they were rebellious and grieved his holy spirit" [Isa. 63:9–10]. When were those "whom he exalted throughout all the days of this age" rebellious? When did they "grieve his holy spirit"?

(7) Consider another instance in which God openly promises to one body both enduring strength and destruction. First he says: "Jerusalem is a rich city, tents that will not be moved; the pegs of your tent will never be pulled up, nor will its ropes be severed"; but then he continues: "Your ropes are severed because the mast of your ship was not strong; your sails hang idly, and the ship will not raise anchor until it is left to perish" [Isa. 33:20, 23].

(8) Again, that the Body of Christ is bipartite is shown in this brief sentence: "I am dark and beautiful" [Song of Sol. 1:5]. I cannot think for a moment that the church "without spot or wrinkle" [Eph. 5:27], whom the Lord "cleansed for himself by his blood" [Titus 2:14], should be dark anywhere except on her left side by which "the name of God is blasphemed among the Gentiles" [Rom. 2:24]. Otherwise she is entirely beautiful, as the author himself says later: "You are all beautiful, my most beloved, and there is no blemish in you" [Song of Sol. 4:7]. Our text gives an explanation of why she is both dark and beautiful: "like the tent of Kedar, like the leather tent of Solomon" [Song of Sol. 1:5]. It shows us two tents, the king's and the slave's; yet both are Abraham's offspring, for Kedar is the son of Ishmael. Elsewhere, the church bemoans her long sojourn with this same Kedar, that is, with the slave from Abraham: "Woe is me

that my wandering has been made long; I have dwelt amid the tents of Kedar, my soul has wandered much. I kept peace with those who hate peace; when I spoke to them, they made war on me" [Ps. 119:5–7, LXX]. Nevertheless, we cannot say that the tent of Kedar is outside the church. Our text speaks of the tent of Kedar and of Solomon, and therefore it says both: "I am dark" and "I am beautiful." But the church herself is not dark because of those who belong outside.

(9) In the same mysterious fashion the Lord mentions seven angels in the Book of Revelation, pointing to a sevenfold church [Rev. 1:20—3:22]; sometimes its members are saints and keepers of the commandments, sometimes they are guilty of numerous sins and need to repent. In the Gospel, he attributes various kinds of merit to one body of stewards, saying first: "Blessed is that servant whom his master, when he comes, shall find so doing," but continuing about the same person: "but when that wicked servant . . ." and adding: "The Lord will divide him in two parts" [Matt. 24:48, 51]. I ask, will the Lord divide or cut him up as a whole? Note the final statement: "He will give him a part"—not the whole!—"with the hypocrites" [v. 51]. Thus, in the one person, the text points to a (bipartite) body.

(10) Therefore, all the statements throughout Scripture in which God announces that Israel will perish deservedly or that his inheritance will be cursed must be understood in terms of this mystery. The apostle makes ample use of this mode of expression, especially in Romans; statements about a whole body must be understood to apply to a part only: "What does God say to Israel? All the day long I stretched out my hands to a contradictory people" [Rom. 10:21]. In order to make it clear that he is speaking of a part only, he continues: "I say then, has God rejected his inheritance? By no means! For I also am an Israelite of the seed of Abraham, of the tribe of Benjamin. God has not rejected his people whom he foreknew" [Rom. 11:1–2]. And having set forth the correct understanding of this statement, he uses the same mode of expression to show us that the one body is both good and evil: "As regards the gospel, they are enemies for your sake; but as regards election, they are beloved for the sake of the fathers" [Rom. 11:28]. Are the beloved the

same as the enemies? Can both terms apply to Caiaphas? Thus, the Lord testifies in all of Scripture that the one body of Abraham's seed is growing and flourishing, but also perishing in all (its various parts).

III. Of Promises and the Law

(1) Divine authority tells us that no one has ever been able to achieve justification by works of the law. The same authority asserts in the strongest terms that there have always been people who kept the law and were justified.

It is written: "Whatever the law says, it is speaking to those who are under the law, so that every mouth may be stopped and the whole world may become subject to God. For by the law no flesh shall be justified in his sight" [Rom. 3:19–20]; and: "Sin shall have no dominion over you, since you are not under the law" [Rom. 6:14]; and: "We also believe in Christ, that we may be justified by faith and not by the works of the law, for by the works of the law no flesh will be justified" [Gal. 3:16]; and: "For if a law had been given that could bestow life, righteousness would certainly be by the law. But Scripture confined all things under sin, that by the faith of Jesus Christ the promise might be given to those who believe" [Gal. 3:21–23]. Now someone might say: From Christ's time onward, the law does not justify; it did, however, justify in its own time. But this argument is contradicted by the authority of the apostle Peter who, when his colleagues were trying to force the Gentiles under the yoke of the law, said: "Why do you test the Lord by trying to impose on the neck of the disciples a yoke which neither our fathers nor we have been able to bear?" [Acts 15:10]. The apostle Paul states: "While we were in the flesh, the sinful passions which come through the law were at work in our members to bear fruit for death" [Rom. 7:5]. Yet, contrary to this, the same apostle also writes: "As regards the righteousness of the law, (I was) leading a blameless life" [Phil. 3:6]. And if the authority of such a great apostle were lacking, how could one criticize the testimony of the Lord who said (of Nathanael): "Behold, a true Israelite in whom there is no guile" [John 1:47]? And even if the Lord had not seen fit to furnish this testimony, who would be so impious, so inflated by senseless pride as to assert that Moses, the prophets, and all the saints (of old) did not fulfill the law or were not justified? Scripture itself says of Zechariah and his wife: "They were both righteous in God's sight, walking in all his commandments and justifications blameless" [Luke 1:6]; and our Lord did not come "to call the righteous, but sinners" [Matt. 9:13].

(2) But how could a law justify from sin when it was given for the purpose of multiplying sin as it is written: "The law came in, so that sin might be multiplied" [Rom. 5:20]? There is one thing we must know and keep in mind: To this very day, the seed of Abraham has never been entirely cut off from Isaac; I am speaking not of the carnal, but of the spiritual seed of Abraham which does not come from the law but from promise. The other seed is indeed carnal; it comes from the law, "from Mount Sinai which is Hagar, bearing children for slavery" [Gal. 4:24]; "the son of the slave woman was born carnally, the son of the free woman by virtue of the promise" [v. 23]. The apostle even states that there is no seed of Abraham but the one which comes from faith: "So you see, that those who are from faith are the children of Abraham" [Gal. 3:7]; and: "But you, brethren, like Isaac, are children of the promise" [Gal. 4:28].

(3) Thus, the seed of Abraham comes not from the law but from the promise and has remained uninterrupted from Isaac on. But if it is a fact that Abraham's seed existed before the law and is that seed which comes from faith, then it is also a fact that it never came from the law. It cannot come both from the law and from faith, for law and faith are quite different. The law is not a law of faith but of works, as Scripture says: "The law does not rest on faith; rather, he who does these things shall live by them" [Gal. 3:12]. Therefore, Abraham always had children by faith, but never by the law. "For not through the law but through the righteousness of faith was the promise given to Abraham or his seed, that he should be heir of the world. For if they are heirs who are heirs through the law, faith is made empty and the promise void; for the law works wrath" [Rom. 4:13–15]. Therefore, if faith and the promise to Abraham cannot be abolished at all, the promise has been in force continu-

ously from its inception. Even the giving of the law did not hinder children being born to Abraham by faith according to the promise. The apostle states that the law, given 430 years later, neither impeded nor annulled the promise [Gal. 3:17]: "For if (the inheritance) is from the law, it is no longer from the promise. But God gave it to Abraham by promise" [v. 18]; and later: "Is then the law contrary to the promise? By no means!" [v. 21]. We see that the law does not touch the promise. Rather than impinging upon one another, each of the two preserves its own order. For just as the law never hindered faith, so faith never destroyed the law. We read: "Do we therefore through faith destroy the law? By no means! Rather we establish the law" [Rom. 3:31], that is, we strengthen it, for the two strengthen each other.

(4) Thus, children of Abraham do not come from the law but from faith through the promise. But in taking seriously the denial of their justification by the works of the law, we must ask how they were justified once they were placed under the law and were observing it. We must ask further why, after the promise of faith which cannot be annulled, the law was given at all, a law not based on faith, a law whose works do not justify anyone. For "all who rely on the works of the law are under a curse, since it is written: Cursed is everyone who does not abide by all things written in the book of the law to do them" [Gal. 3:10]. The apostle anticipates this question. While asserting uncompromisingly that there have always been children of Abraham by God's grace through faith, not through the law of deeds, he makes this objection to himself: "Why then the law of deeds?" [Gal. 3:19]. That is to say: If there are children by virtue of faith, why was the law of deeds given, when the promise was sufficient to produce children of Abraham and to nourish them in faith, since "he who is righteous lives by faith"? Even before posing the question, "why then the law of deeds?", he stated that those who cannot be justified by virtue of the law will live in that other manner: "By the law no one is justified before God, but he who is righteous lives by faith" [Gal. 3:11]. He points out that the prophet said "He who is righteous lives by faith," precisely because it should be made clear how those unable to fulfill the law might live.

(5) The meaning of the phrase, "he who is righteous lives by faith," is less clear. For a righteous person, placed under the law, can only live if he performs the works of the law, indeed all its works, otherwise he would be cursed. God gave the law. He said: "You shall not covet." But immediately "sin, finding an opportunity, wrought every kind of covetousness by means of the commandment" [Rom. 7:7–8], for "the sinful passions which come through the law" [v. 5] are inevitably at work in the members of anyone under the law. The law was given "so that sin might abound" [Rom. 5:20], because "the power of sin is the law" [1 Cor. 15:56]. Now anyone sold under sin does not do the good that he wants, but the very evil he does not want. According to his inner self he consents to the law, but is overpowered by another law in his members [Rom. 7:14–23]. Dragged along captive, he can never be freed except by grace alone, through faith. But there is one kind of weapon which can check the violence of sin; failure to heed it is a great crime of faithlessness; to seek and identify it, on the other hand, is the sign of a marvelous faith. A mind realizing that humans cannot possibly fulfill the law which stands ready to take revenge, and yet failing to understand that there is a life-giving remedy, is nothing less than perverse and blasphemous. It simply is not possible that a good God, knowing that the law cannot be fulfilled, should provide no other access to life and close off all roads to life for human beings whom he created for life. Faith cannot bear or admit this thought; instead, when it is beset by the weakness of the flesh and the power of sin, it gives God the glory. Knowing that the Lord is good and just, and that he does not close the depths of his mercy against the works of his hands, faith realizes that there *is* a way to life and sees a remedy enabling us to fulfill the law. In the words "you shall not covet," God did not reveal how this might be done successfully. He simply said sternly and tersely: "You shall not covet," leaving the rest to be discovered by faith. If he had commanded that we ask him for the result, he would have destroyed both the law and faith. For why would God even give the law if he had already promised to fulfill the law in each and every person? And what would he leave to faith, if his promise of assistance already preceded it? God gave the law as an agent of death for the good of faith; those who love

life should see life by faith, and the righteous should live by faith, believing that they cannot do the work of the law by virtue of their own strength but only by virtue of God's gift. The law cannot be fulfilled by the flesh; it punishes everything that is left undone.

(6) How then can a human being hope to fulfill the law and escape death except by God's rich mercy, which only faith can discover? "The flesh does not submit to the law of God, indeed it cannot; for those who are in the flesh cannot please God. But you are not in the flesh, you are in the spirit, if indeed the Spirit of God dwells in you. But if anyone does not have the Spirit of Christ, he does not belong to him" [Rom. 8:7–9]. Paul makes the point that the Spirit of God and of Christ is the same. He points out also that the one who has the Spirit of God is not in the flesh. But if God's Spirit and Christ's Spirit is one and the same, then the prophets and saints who had God's Spirit also had the Spirit of Christ. Since they had the Spirit of God, they were not in the flesh. Since they were not in the flesh, they fulfilled the law, for the flesh is at enmity with God and does not submit to his law. Therefore, anyone who flees to God receives God's Spirit, and once the Spirit is received, the flesh is put to death. Once the flesh is put to death, one can fulfill the law as a spiritual person, freed from the law, for "the law is not laid down for the righteous" [1 Tim. 1:9], and: "If you are led by God's Spirit, you are not under the law" [Gal. 5:18].

(7) It is therefore quite clear that our forefathers, who had God's Spirit, were not under the law. As long as one is in the flesh, that is, without God's Spirit, the law is in command. But by surrendering to grace, one dies to the law; now the Spirit fulfills the law in one's person while the flesh, unable to submit to the law of God, is dead. What went on before is still going on now. The commandment prohibiting covetousness has not ceased to be valid because we are no longer under the law, nor has it been made more severe. But we seek refuge through faith in the revealed grace; being taught by the Lord to ask for our doing of the law as a gift of his mercy, we pray: "Your will be done," and "deliver us from evil" [Matt. 6:10, 13]. The fathers acted by this same faith, though it was the fear of death that

compelled them to seek a grace not yet revealed; through the agency of the law, they saw death threatening them with its sword drawn.

(8) The law was given "until the time, when the seed to whom the promise was made would come" [Gal. 3:19] and proclaim the good news of faith. Before this time, however, it was the law that drove people toward faith; for faith as the search for God's grace cannot be expressed without the law, because sin would have no power. But once the law was given, "the passions which come through the law were at work in our members" [Rom. 7:5], forcing us into sin and driving us necessarily toward faith, which would cry out for God's grace to help us endure. We were kept in prison, while the law threatened death and surrounded us with an insurmountable wall wherever we turned. Grace was the one and only door in this wall. Faith was the guard in charge of this door, so that no one could escape from the prison unless faith opened the door. Failure to knock at this door meant dying within the walls of the law. We suffered under the law as under a tutor who drove us to be eager for faith, and thus drove us to Christ. The apostle says that the law was given that it should confine us by its custody toward the faith which was to be revealed as faith in Christ, who is "the end of the law" [Rom. 10:4]; he is the one by whom all who have sought the grace of God by faith have found their life: "Before faith came, we were kept under the law, confined unto that faith which was to be revealed. Thus, the law was our tutor in Christ that we might be justified by faith" [Gal. 3:23–24].

(9) I said that the law demonstrated the need for faith. But someone might object: If the law was given to benefit faith, why did its giving not coincide with the beginning of Abraham's seed, if it was constantly present? Indeed, it was there all the time. Faith was continuously present, giving birth to the children of Abraham, and so was the law, in the ability to discern good and evil. But once the promise of children had been given to Abraham, and his seed according to the flesh was growing in numbers, his seed from faith had to grow also. Now this expansion could not occur without the help of an expanded law, so that an ever greater multitude would be led almost by necessity

to a faith not yet revealed, as I pointed out above. Thus, it was an act of God's providence for the increase and guidance of the seed of Abraham, that the severity and fear of the law drove many to faith and strengthened the seed until faith was revealed. "The law came in, so that sin might be multiplied. But where sin was multiplied, grace abounded yet more" [Rom. 5:20]. Paul did not say: "grace was given," but: "grace abounded yet more." For through Christ it had been given from the beginning to those who sought refuge from the vexations and the domination of the law. Grace was already abundant through the expansion of the law, but it abounded yet more when it was revealed to all flesh in Christ. He came to "restore things in heaven and things on earth" [Eph. 1:10] and announced faith as the "good tidings to those nearby and those far off" [Eph. 2:17], that is, both to the sinners of Israel and to the Gentiles. Those Israelites who were righteous by virtue of faith had already been called to the same faith. For the Spirit, the faith, and the grace given by Christ have always been the same. By his coming, Christ bestowed the fullness of these gifts upon the whole race, having removed the veil of the law. The difference between their earlier and their later bestowal was one of degree, not of kind. By other means there never was a seed of Abraham.

(10) Justification apart from these gifts did not make anyone a child of Abraham. A man cannot be called a son of Abraham if he is justified by virtue of the law, not by virtue of faith like Abraham. Indeed, the apostle teaches that the church passed from one image of grace and spirit into the very same, when he writes: "But we all with unveiled faces, reflecting as in a mirror the glory of God, are being changed into the same image from glory to glory" [2 Cor. 3:18]. He implies that there was glory even before the Lord's passion and denies that such glory could be extracted, that is, expressed, brought forth, or effected from the law. Thus, glory was obviously coming from faith. "Where then is the boasting?" he asks. "It is excluded. By what law? By the law of works? No, but by the law of faith" [Rom. 3:27]. "For what does scripture say? Abraham believed God, and it was reckoned to him as righteousness" [Rom. 4:3]. We have passed

into glory from the same glory, which did not come from the law. Had it been based on works, it would have been glory, but not glory given to God [cf. v. 2].

(11) To repeat: It is impossible to have any glory without the grace of God. There is only one glory, and it has always been of one kind. No human being has ever triumphed for whom God has not won the victory. This is not so under the law; there, the one who fulfills it is the victor. But under faith it is God who renders our adversary powerless, so that "he who glories should glory in the Lord" [1 Cor. 1:31]. For since the victory is not ours, it is not achieved by works but by faith, and there is nothing of ourselves in which to glory. We have nothing that we have not received [cf. 1 Cor. 4:7]. If we exist, we have our existence from God, so that the greatness of power may be God's and not ours. All our work is faith, and it is as great as God working with us. Solomon glories in the knowledge that continence does not come from a human source but is a gift of God: "Knowing that I could not be continent unless God granted it— and this itself is wisdom, to know whose gift it is—I went to the Lord and besought him" [Wisd. of Sol. 8:21]. We must accept the judgment of Solomon that all the justified exist by the grace of God, not by virtue of works. They know that the doing of the law in which they can glory must be requested from God. The apostle, however, clarifies why no flesh should glory before God; the wicked, of course, because they do not know God, and the righteous because they are not their own work but God's. He writes: "God chose what is useless and discarded, even things that are not, to bring to nothing things that are, so that no flesh might glory before God. From him you are in Christ Jesus, who has become for us the wisdom from God, our righteousness, holiness, and redemption; therefore, as it is written: Let him who glories, glory in the Lord" [1 Cor. 1:28–31]; and: "By grace you have been saved through faith, and this is not your doing, it is the gift of God; not because of works, lest anyone should boast. For we are his handiwork, created in Christ" [Eph. 2:8–10].

(12) Therefore, no flesh can ever be justified by virtue of the law, that is, by works, so that any righteous person may have his

glory from God. There is another reason why no one should boast before God. God works with his own in such a way that there is always something for him to forgive; for "no one is free from defilement, though his life were only one day long" [Job 14:4–5?]. David pleads: "Enter not into judgment with your servant, for before you no man living is justified" [Ps. 142:2, LXX]. And Solomon prays at the dedication of the Temple: "For there is no one who does not sin" [1 Kings 8:46]. Also: "Against you alone have I sinned" [Ps. 50:6, LXX], and: "Who can boast to have a pure heart, or who can boast to be clean from sin?" [Prov. 20:9]. To speak of a pure heart, that is, of freedom from evil thoughts, is not enough; it must be added that no one should boast to be clean from sin! Every victory is granted by God's sheer mercy, not by virtue of works, as it is written: "He crowns you with mercy and compassion" [Ps. 102:4, LXX]. The mother of the (Maccabean) martyrs said to her son: "In that mercy, may I receive you again with your brothers" [2 Macc. 7:29]. The righteous perfect the will of God through their prayer and effort by which they strive and desire to serve God.

(13) The law leaves no room for good and better; if it could justify, all the righteous would have shared one merit because it demands equal observance of all its precepts. If one did less, the curse would become effective. But if the righteous showed unequal merit, each person receiving as much of the merciful God's grace as his faith told him he had been given, they were transformed "from glory into glory, as through the Spirit of the Lord" [2 Cor. 3:18], that is, from one state into more of the same state. After Christ, the gift of faith was the same in kind as the Holy Spirit, since every prophet and righteous one always lived by the same Spirit. They could not live otherwise but by the Spirit of faith. For all who were under the law were killed because "the letter kills but the Spirit makes alive" [2 Cor. 3:6]. And yet the Lord said of the same Spirit: "If I do not go away, he will not come" [John 16:7], though he had already given this very Spirit to his apostles. The apostle expresses the fact that the same Spirit was with the ancient generations in these words: "Because we have the same Spirit of faith, as it is written: I believed, and so I spoke" [2 Cor. 4:13]. He implies that the one

who said, "I believed, and so I spoke," had this same Spirit of faith, and he confirms it by adding: "We too believe, and so we also speak." By saying "we too" he makes clear that the ancient generations believed through the same Spirit of faith. Thus it is obvious that the righteous have always had their gifts not by virtue of the law but through the Spirit of faith.

(14) Whatever comes through the Lord is a whole whose every part is from the same author. Think of a young boy. He has nothing less than a man, but he is not yet a man; full bodily stature comes to him by the growth not of new members but of the ones that are already there. Still, the person who has reached perfection is the same one who was a small boy. In the full and proper sense, the Holy Spirit "was not yet" before the Lord's passion [John 7:39]. But he existed in those who had faith through him being present so that, sealed by him, the victor and perfector of all things, they might reach perfection. Clearly the righteous people whom Christ met already possessed the Holy Spirit—men and women like Simeon and Nathanael, Zechariah and Elizabeth, and the widow Anna, the daughter of Phanuel.

(15) Therefore, the promise is independent of the law, and since it is something so different, the two cannot be mixed; for any condition weakens the promise. At this point I am forced to say things which I cannot hear without the burn of deep pain. Some people who are ignorant about the firmness of the promise and about the transgression brought on by the law maintain that God promised Abraham all the nations, but did so without prejudice to their free will—under the condition that they would keep the law. Now it may be useful for their own salvation to expose the dangers which the inexperience of certain people breeds. But if our topic is the omnipotent God, we must exercise restraint in what we say so that we do not mention what ought to be passed over in silence and allow unworthy things to be heard from our lips. I speak, therefore, with some trembling and leave to each side the consideration of its own dangers.

(16) God obviously knew beforehand whether those whom he promised to Abraham would exist of their own free will or not. There are two options: Either they would; in this case, the

question is settled. Or they would not; in this case, the God who gave the promise did not keep his word. If it was God's decision to give the promised (nations) if and when they were willing, God certainly would have said so in order to prevent games from being played on his servant Abraham, who believed that "what God has promised, he is able also to do" [Rom. 4:21]. God's promise does not allow any condition; else the promise would not be firm, nor would faith retain its integrity. For how could God's promise or Abraham's faith remain stable if that which was promised and believed depended upon the choice of the promised ones? God would have been promising something that was not his, and Abraham would have believed incautiously. How then was it possible that the promise turned into nothing less than an obligation very soon, when God said: "In you all the nations of the earth shall be blessed because you have listened to my voice and have not withheld your own beloved son from me" [Gen. 22:18, 16]? Now some people find it easy to taunt Abraham's merit with the calumny of free choice on the basis of these texts; so God confirmed his debt to Abraham once more after Abraham's death, promising his son what he was going to do on Abraham's account. These are his words: "I will be with you and will bless you; for to you and your seed I will give this land, and I will fulfill the oath which I swore to your father Abraham. I will multiply your seed like the stars of heaven and will give all the nations of the earth to you and your seed, because your father Abraham listened to my voice" [Gen. 26:3–5]. Thus the debt to Abraham was confirmed, for Abraham could not lose after his death through someone's free choice what he had merited while he was alive.

(17) But the nations were not willing to believe. What could Abraham do being owed this debt? How was he to collect the debt owed to his faith and trial? He was certain of it, since God was his debtor. If God had said to him: "I will give what I promised and deliver on my oath if the nations are willing," Abraham would not have believed but taken a chance. If there must be a condition, it can apply to the laborer only but not to the wages. The laborer may or may not be willing to accept payment, but this does not go for the wages. All the nations were given to

Abraham as wages of faith. God said: "Your wages are great" [Gen. 15:1]. God did not make his promise on the condition that they would exist; nor did he make it because they were going to exist. If it was God's good pleasure to save all nations, it was not on account of Abraham's faith at all; they were God's possession not only before Abraham's faith, but before the foundation of the world. Rather, God sought a faithful person to whom he wished to give that from which would come what he had determined would exist anyway. Thus, Abraham did not merit the existence of those future nations, whom God had elected and foreknown to become conformed to the image of his Son [Rom. 8:29], as such; rather, he merited their existence *through him*. Scripture testifies in Genesis that God promised all nations to Abraham on the basis of his foreknowledge: "Surely Abraham shall and will become a great and numerous nation, and all the nations of the earth shall be blessed in him." For God "knew that Abraham charged his sons and his household after him, and they were going to observe the ways of the Lord, exercising righteousness and judgment, so that the Lord might bring upon Abraham all that he had told him" [Gen. 18:18–19].

(18) But we also encounter conditions, for instance: "If you listen to me and are willing" [Isa. 1:19]. Where is God's foreknowledge, where is his firm promise in such conditions? The apostle said that the promise was given by virtue of faith, not of the law, precisely in order that it might stand firm. "The law," he said, "works wrath, for where there is no law neither is there transgression. Therefore, the promise was by virtue of faith, that it might be firm for all the seed according to grace" [Rom. 4:15–16]. "That the promise might be firm" is correct, for with a condition attached to it the promise would not be firm. It is rather foolish and arrogant to believe that something addressed to the bipartite body applies to the whole body. God could not say, "*if* you hear me," to those who he knew would hear, when he had known even before he made them that they would remain in the image of God; he could not say this to the very seed which was promised. The condition, that is, the law, was given for the impious and sinners only [cf. 1 Tim. 1:9], so that

they might either flee to grace or receive punishment more justly if they robbed grace of its effect. Why should the law apply to the righteous for whom it was not made, who fulfill the law without the law because God is gracious, who serve God freely and live according to the image of God and Christ? They are good by their own volition. The person under the law may not be an open murderer for fear of death, but he is not merciful; he does not bear the image of God. He does not like the law, but he fears its revenge. He cannot fulfill what he thinks he ought to do if he does it out of necessity rather than by his own decision. He has no choice but to fall back on his own will, which means that he will receive the sure reward of the one who has not fused his soul with the will of God. What God wills is not to his liking. In fact, someone who is good only out of necessity has an evil will. The law curbs the deed, not the will. Someone who would embrace evil if there were no penalty for it is not in tune with God. Complaining that one cannot do one's own will is not equivalent to doing God's will. The fear of being cruel does not make one merciful; such a person is under the law, is a slave. He does not detest stealing but only fears punishment. But he must do his stealing persuaded and convinced, because he is a carnal being under the power of sin and does not have the Spirit of God. On the other hand, he who loves what is good bears the image of God and lives by faith in the Lord; in him the heir is no longer the son of the slave woman, receiving the law in fear. Rather, like Isaac, he is the son of the free woman, the one who "has not received a spirit of slavery so as to be again in fear, but a spirit of adoption as sons crying Abba, Father" [Rom. 8:15]. He who loves God is not fearful like a slave. It is written: "There is no fear in love, but perfect love casts out fear, because fear brings punishment; he who fears is not consummated in love" [1 John 4:18]. Servile fear is coupled with hatred of discipline; but a son's fear goes together with the honor of the father.

(19) To live in fear because of the law is one thing, but to honor God out of veneration for his awesome majesty is another. People who do the latter resemble their Father who is in heaven; reminded by him and taught, they love the good and hate evil. They do not shun evil out of fear; they do not do good

out of necessity. They are without a law; they are free; they are the promised ones. "If you hear me" is not addressed to them. Those to whom it is, may choose not to hear. Can the phrase apply to one of whom God foreknew before the world began that he would hear? True, even the righteous "whom God foreknew" [Rom. 8:20] live under this law. They also are addressed by these words, "if you hear me," but for a different reason; not because they may choose not to hear, but so that they may always be solicitous for their salvation, since they do not know their end. Indeed, no one is certain of belonging to the number of the foreknown; even the apostle is concerned "lest I myself be rejected" [1 Cor. 9:27]. For the righteous, therefore, that law does not work wrath, but it exercises their faith. It is by faith that they must constantly seek God's grace while they are laboring, so that what God foresaw in them might be perfected, and they might be destined for life by their own free choice. In any other sense it is impossible that the one who God foresaw, promised, and even swore would hear, should not hear.

(20) In the Gospel the Lord explains to which part the law properly applies even though it is given to the one body. He says to the apostles: "If you know these things, blessed are you if you do them. I do not speak of you all; I know whom I have chosen" [John 13:17–18]. What admirable brevity! He points out the one body, and at the same time divides it. If he had said: "I do not speak of you," or: "I do not speak of all," he would not point out the one body. But by saying, "I do not speak of you all," he makes it clear that, even though he is not speaking of them all, he is speaking nonetheless of them. It is as if someone said: "I am not speaking of your whole person." Two bodies are mingled as if they were one, and the one body is praised or rebuked in common. This is like God's words addressed to Moses in Exodus, after some Israelites had gone out to collect manna against the Sabbath prohibition: "How long do you refuse to obey my law?" [Exod. 16:28]; in fact, Moses himself had always obeyed.

(21) But what shall we say of a law that seems openly opposed to the promise? In Isaiah, we read: "If you had hearkened to me, O Israel, your number would be like the sand of the sea" [Isa.

48:18–19]. Here, Israel is rebuked for not having become like the sand through its own fault. The inference must be that, if it will always fail to hearken, it will always remain small in number. Now where is the firmness of the promises? The problem is our wish to understand before we believe; we want to subjugate faith to reason. If we firmly believe that things come to pass entirely as God has sworn, then faith will give a reason which reason would find faithless to question. We will then understand that there is more firmness to the promise than infirmity, as we tend to think. For the statement, "if you had hearkened to me, O Israel," is a reminder of God's righteousness and a confirmation of his promises; no one should dare to think that not by their free choice but by God's disposition some are destined for death and others for life. God said to the generation then living: "If you had hearkened to me," in order to leave no doubt after the giving of the promise that they would be like sand; he did foresee others who would listen. When anything was said about this matter before the time of our Lord Jesus Christ, the seed of Abraham was not yet like the sand of the sea. This is easy to prove. First, because God promised this large number in Christ only: "Not to seeds, referring to many, but referring to one: 'and to your seed,' which is Christ" [Gal. 3:16]. Second, because he promised all nations, and this promise could not be fulfilled before Christ. If the number of the children of Israel really was like the sand of the sea even before the Lord's coming, it included the false brethren who are not children of Abraham; for not all who are from Abraham are children of Abraham, and not all who are from Israel are Israel. When the apostle "wished to be accursed" for the sake of Israel, "who possessed the adoption as sons and the covenants" [Rom. 9:3–4], he made it very clear that he did not mean those (false) children of Abraham; rather, because of his love for them out of fleshly necessity, he deplored the fact that they did not belong to that number; he did not imply that God's promise had failed: "It is not as though the word of God had failed. For not all who are descended from Israel are Israel, neither are they all children because they are the seed of Abraham; but in Isaac shall your seed be named. This means that it is not the children of the flesh who are the children of God, but the children of the promise are reckoned as the seed" [Rom. 9:6–8].

(22) In the multitude of ancient Israel, therefore, the only seed of Abraham were those who, like Isaac, were children of faith and of promise. Paul gives a further example: "Though the number of the children of Israel be as the sand of the sea, only a remnant shall be saved" [Rom. 9:27], that is, a small part. And: "If the Lord of hosts had not left us a seed, we would be like Sodom" [Rom. 9:29]. This remnant was the seed of Abraham, so that not all of Judea would be like Sodom. Again, Paul claims that God never abandoned his inheritance; rather, the situation has always been what it was at the time of the Lord's coming, when only part of Israel was saved; he writes: "What is the answer? 'I have kept for myself seven thousand men who have not bowed their knees to Baal.' Even so now, a remnant has been saved, according to the election of grace" [Rom. 11:4–5]. By saying, "even so now, at the present time," he points out that it had always been this way in Israel: a remnant, that is, a small number, was saved.

(23) If, however, neither faith nor reason make a persuasive case, there are still the words addressed to him who was promised: "If you had hearkened to me, O Israel, your number would be like the sand of the sea" [Isa. 48:18–19]. The same Jacob who had been chosen even before he was born was later rejected through his own free choice, as Hosea says: "The judgment of the Lord is upon Judah that he will punish Jacob for his conduct and repay him for his pursuits. For in the womb he cheated his brother, and by his labors he stood up to God and stood up to the angel and became powerful" [Hos. 12:2–4]. Now if it is true that God's beloved reached fullness in Jacob, then the one who "by his labors stood up to God" and the "cheater" are not one and the same, but two in one body. What we have here is a figure of the twofold seed of Abraham, that is, of the two peoples struggling in the one womb of Mother Church. One of them is beloved according to the election by God's foreknowledge, the other wicked by the election of his own will. Jacob and Esau exist in one body from one seed. The clear fact that two were generated demonstrates that there are two peoples.

(24) Lest someone think, however, that the separation of the two peoples is so clear, it was arranged for both to exist in one body, in Jacob, who was called both "beloved" and "cheater of his brother." Therefore, the two express the quantity, not the quality of the separation. One further point is made: The two who are separated will be present in one before there is a division. Isaac said: "Your brother came with cunning and took your blessing" [Gen. 27:35]. Now this may be a mystical expression by which (the author) briefly hints at the two in one body. But is it not contrary to reason that the cunning one should receive the blessing meant for his neighbor, when even Scripture says: "He who does not swear to his neighbor with cunning will receive a blessing from the Lord" [Ps. 23:4–5, LXX]? In fact, Jacob, that is, the church, never came and took the blessing without the accompaniment of cunning, that is, of false brethren. But even if innocence and cunning come to take the blessing together, this does not mean that they are blessed together; for only "he who can take it, takes" [Matt. 19:12]. One seed only, because of the quality of its soil, grows up.

(25) If the text does not say: "In the womb he cheated Esau," but: (he cheated) "his brother," this does not contradict the fact that he cheated a wicked brother. Esau is the symbol and the designation for the wicked everywhere, while Jacob stands for both because the bad part pretends to be Jacob; thus the two appear under one name. But the good part cannot pretend to be Esau. Therefore, the latter is the name for wicked people only, while the former is bipartite. Moreover, by his free choice Jacob does not include all the good seed, nor Esau all the bad; but both kinds come from both of them. Abraham's seed was twofold; this is the point. One of his sons was born of a slave woman figuratively in order to show that slaves, too, would come from Abraham. This son went away with his mother. But after he was gone, the one who received the law "on Mount Sinai, which is Hagar, bringing forth children for slavery" [Gal. 4:24], was found even in the seed of the other, coming from the free woman, from Israel. There, in the same people, children of the promise like Isaac, saints, and believers were generated in large numbers from the free woman. Thus, even when the figurative Ishmael

and Esau were separated from the believers, still the whole (process) resulted in one people later on. From the beginning both covenants, that of Hagar and that of Isaac, lay hidden and still lie hidden in it, even though for a time one appeared under the name of the other, because the old covenant did not stop generating when the new one was revealed. Scripture does not say: "Hagar who bore children in her old age," but: "which is Hagar, bearing children for slavery."

(26) Both, however, must "grow together until the harvest" [Matt. 13:30]. In the past, the new covenant revealed in Christ lay hidden under the proclamation of the old covenant—(the new covenant of) grace which would generate children of the promise, like Isaac, from the free woman. In the same way, now that the new covenant prevails, there is no lack of children of slavery born of Hagar, as Christ's appearance as judge will reveal. The apostle confirms this picture: The struggle of the brothers continues even now, the same struggle which went on between them in the past: "You brethren, like Isaac, are children of the promise. But just as at that time he who was born according to the flesh persecuted the spiritual one, so it is now also," and he adds the necessary conclusion: "What does scripture say? Cast out the slave woman and her son, for the son of the slave woman shall not be heir with the son of the free woman" [Gal. 4:28–29]. The wording here is not without significance: "Just as he persecuted, so it is now also." "He persecuted" is the apostle's interpretation. For Scripture says: "Ishmael was playing with Isaac" [Gen. 21:9]. The false brethren who were preaching circumcision to the Galatians did not attack them openly. Did they not rather attack playfully, that is, without the signs of open persecution? Paul calls the "playing" Ishmael a persecutor. He does the same with those who are striving to separate the children of God from Christ and to make them children of their mother Hagar by appealing as if to the common welfare, namely, the discipline of the law.

(27) The only reason the children of the devil slip in "to spy upon our liberty" [Gal. 2:4], pretend to be brothers, and play in our paradise like children of God, is their desire to glory in the suppression of the freedom of the children of God. "They incur

131

the judgment, whoever they are" [Gal. 5:10]; they persecute every saint, they kill the prophets [cf. Matt. 23:37], they "always resist the Holy Spirit" [Acts 7:51]. As "enemies of the cross of Christ" [Phil. 3:18], "denying Christ in the flesh" [1 John 4:3] while hating his members, they are "the body of sin, the son of perdition" revealing the "mystery of iniquity" [2 Thess. 2:3, 7]. They are the ones whose coming is "according to the working of Satan with all power and signs and false miracles" [v. 9], "spiritual forces of wickedness on high" [Eph. 6:12]. Christ the Lord, whom they persecute in the flesh, will "slay them with the breath of his mouth and will destroy them by the manifestation of his coming" [2 Thess. 2:8]. For now is the time in which these things should be set out openly, not in riddles, the time when that departure which is the revelation of the man of sin is imminent, the time when Lot leaves Sodom.

ᵀBibliography

PRIMARY SOURCES

Sifra. *Sifra: Der älteste Midrasch zu Levitikus,* edited by M. Fried-
mann, Schriften der Gesellschaft zur Förderung des Judentums.
Breslau: M. and H. Marcus, 1915.

Ptolemy. *Ptolemée: Lettre à Flora,* 2d ed., edited by G. Quispel,
Sources chrétiennes, no. 24. Paris: Editions du Cerf, 1967.

Irenaeus. *Irénée de Lyon. Contre les Hérésies, Livre IV. Tome II: Texte
et traduction,* edited by A. Rousseau, Sources chrétiennes, no. 100.
Paris: Editions du Cerf, 1965.

Origen. *Origène, Traité des principes. Tome III (livres III et IV),*
edited by H. Crouzel and M. Simonetti, Sources chrétiennes, no.
268. Paris: Editions du Cerf, 1980.

Origen. *Origenes Vier Bücher von den Prinzipien,* edited by H.
Görgemanns and H. Karpp, Texte zur Forschung, Band 24. Darm-
stadt: Wissenschaftliche Buchgesellschaft, 1976.

Papyrus Michigan 3718. A. Henrichs and E. M. Husselman, eds.,
"Christian Allegorizations (Pap. Mich. Inv. 3718)," *Zeitschrift für
Papyrologie und Epigraphik* (Bonn) 3 (1968): 175–89.

Diodore of Tarsus. *Diodori Tarsensis Commentarii in Psalmos. I.
Commentarii in Psalmos I – L,* edited by J.-M. Olivier, Corpus
Christianorum, Series Graeca, VI. Turnholti: Typographi Brepols
Editores Pontificii, 1980.

Diodore of Tarsus. Mariès, L., ed., "Extraits du commentaire de
Diodore de Tarse sur les Psaumes: Preface du commentaire—
Prologue du Psaume CXVIII," *Recherches de Science religieuse*
(Paris) 9 (1919): 79–101.

Theodore of Mopsuestia. *Theodore of Mopsuestia. Commentary on
the Epistles of St. Paul. Latin Version with Greek Fragments,* vol. 1,
edited by H. B. Swete, 1880. Reprint. Cambridge: At the University
Press, 1969.

133

Tyconius. *The Book of Rules of Tyconius,* edited by F. C. Burkitt, Texts and Studies, vol. III, no. 1, edited by J. A. Robinson. Cambridge: At the University Press, 1894.

SECONDARY WORKS

The Cambridge History of the Bible. Vol. 1: *From the Beginnings to Jerome,* edited by P.R. Ackroyd and C. F. Evans. New York and Cambridge: Cambridge University Press, 1970.

Campenhausen, H. Frhr. von. *The Formation of the Christian Bible,* translated by J. A. Baker. Philadelphia: Fortress Press, 1972.

Daniélou, J. *From Shadow to Reality: Studies in the Biblical Typology of the Fathers,* translated by W. Hibbard. Westminster, Md.: Newman Press, 1961.

————. *A History of Early Christian Doctrine Before the Council of Nicaea,* translated by J. A. Baker (and D. Smith). Philadelphia: The Westminster Preas.
Vol. 1: *The Theology of Jewish Christianity,* (1964) 1977
Vol. 2: *Gospel Message and Hellenistic Culture,* 1973
Vol. 3: *The Origins of Latin Christianity,* 1977

Daube, D. "Rabbinic Methods of Interpretation and Hellenistic Rhetoric," *Hebrew Union College Annual* (Cincinnati) XXII (1949): 239–64.

Goppelt, L. *Typos. The Typological Interpretation of the Old Testament in the New,* translated by D. H. Madvig. Grand Rapids: Wm. B. Eerdmans, 1982.

Grant, R. M. *The Letter and the Spirit.* New York: Macmillan Co., 1957.

————. *A Short History of the Interpretation of the Bible.* New edition, with update on modern use by D. Tracy. Philadelphia: Fortress Press, 1983.

Greer, R. A. *Theodore of Mopsuestia: Exegete and Theologian.* Westminster, Md.: Faith Press, 1961.

Hanson, R. P. C. *Allegory and Event: A Study of the Sources and Significance of Origen's Interpretation of Scripture.* Richmond: John Knox Press, 1959.

Longenecker, R. N. *Biblical Exegesis in the Apostolic Period.* Grand Rapids: Wm. B. Eerdmans, 1975.

De Lubac, H. *The Sources of Revelation,* translated by Luke O'Neill. New York: Herder & Herder, 1968.

Mielziner, M. *Introduction to the Talmud.* With a new bibliography, 1925–67, by A. Guttmann. New York: Bloch Publishing Co., 1969.

O'Malley, T. P. *Tertullian and the Bible. Language–Imagery–Exegesis.* Latinitas Christianorum Primaeva 21. Nijmegen and Utrecht: Dekker & Van de Vegt, 1967.

Pagels, E. *The Gnostic Paul: Gnostic Exegesis of the Pauline Letters.* Philadelphia: Fortress Press, 1975.

Toblin, T. H. *The Creation of Man: Philo and the History of Interpretation.* The Catholic Biblical Quarterly Monograph Series 14. Washington, D.C.: Catholic Biblical Association of America, 1983.

Trigg, J. W. *Origen: The Bible and Philosophy in the Third-Century Church.* Atlanta: John Knox Press, 1983.

Wallace-Hadrill, D. S. *Christian Antioch. A Study of Early Christian Thought in the East.* New York and Cambridge: Cambridge University Press, 1982.